Cultiv; Human Spirit: Revisiting Maria Montessori's Journey

Punum Bhatia, PhD

MONTESSORI CASA
INTERNATIONAL

144 Rampart Way, Denver, CO 80230

MONTESSORI CASA
INTERNATIONAL

144 Rampart Way, Denver, CO. 80230

©2019

Printed in the USA
ISBN- 13: 978-0-9975938-4-6
All rights reserved

Author: Punum Bhatia, PhD
Editor: Russ Womack
Design: Tim Parker
Cover Illustrator: Kristina Miletic

Photographs by the author, those acknowledged in every chapter, the archives listed in the bibliography, and sources on the internet.

All proceeds from the sale of this book goes to Montessori Casa International, a not-for-profit organization.

Cultivator of the Human Spirit: Revisiting Maria Montessori's Journey

I have now had a chance to read your book and really enjoyed it. It is an interesting travelog tracing the history of Montessori's journeys through her long life.

David Elkind, PhD
Professor Emeritus Tufts University
Author of "The Hurried Child" and "The Power of Play"

Dr. Punum Bhatia makes Montessori philosophy come alive with her travels to places of significance in Maria Montessori's life and her photographs that compare the then and now. The quotes eloquently describe the essence of Montessori, and even 100 years later they are as relevant today as they were then. That in itself is amazing! Just as Dr. Montessori worried then, Dr. Bhatia worries today about the use of the Montessori name being used only to satisfy the adults' goals and not to help the children develop to their full potential. I hope this book will help more educators understand what Montessori is truly about.

Rita Messineo
Student of Adele Costa Gnocchi
Pioneer of the 0-3 Montessori in the USA

Dedicated to understanding and enacting Maria Montessori's philosophy and method with fidelity, Dr. Bhatia provides a delightful, well-researched account of the inspiration and tenacity of a remarkable woman's unfailing dedication to children and the betterment of society.

Nicole Sager, PhD
Culturally and Linguistically Diverse Education
University of Colorado, Denver

Punum Bhatia is a noted Montessori educator and researcher. She is also a true disciple of Maria Montessori, one who looks to the life and original words of the founder to discover and maintain the spirit and underlying theory of the movement. In her latest book, Cultivator of the Spirit: Revisiting Maria Montessori's Journey, Dr. Bhatia becomes a pilgrim, visiting and photographing the places where Montessori lived, wrote, and founded her schools. Her story is a moving tribute to the Montessori movement and its famous founder, beginning as a determined, courageous, and well-grounded alternative to the mind-numbing treatment of Italian working class children at the beginning of the 20th century. The book is also a poignant lesson in how fiercely a woman with a unique vision for educating children had to defend her ideas, her schools, and her movement from being eclipsed or literally taken over by powerful men. Dr. Bhatia follows Montessori as she develops her approach in Italy, captures the attention of wealthy patrons in the United States, puts down roots in Barcelona, and then in Holland, always one step ahead of the spreading influence of fascism in Italy and Spain. Then, as World War II began, Montessori moved to India where she and her movement took on a deepened spiritual perspective where it remains vibrant today. For those of us who can't make this remarkable pilgrimage in person, this book brings it all alive.

Professor Alan Davis
School of Education and Human Development
University of Colorado Denver

Dr. Bhatia's book, *Cultivator of the Human Spirit: Revisiting Maria Montessori's Journey*, provides an in-depth look at the life of Dr. Maria Montessori. The reader is taken on a journey of Dr. Montessori's life from infancy through her death. Dr. Bhatia's personal accounts, interviews, pictures, and research places the reader at the times and locations where this amazing history took place. It provides a deep and rich account of Dr. Montessori's inspiration, beliefs, challenges, and undying commitment to enhancing the lives of young children around the world.

Rosemarie Allen, EdD
Associate Professor Metropolitan State University of Denver

DEDICATION

In honor of my teacher, Maria Montessori, and teachers everywhere who awaken children's curiosity and instill a lifelong love of learning.

TABLE OF CONTENTS

ACKNOWLEDGEMENTS

I am very grateful to all those who have supported me through my Montessori journey and encouraged me to write this book. This would not have been possible without the help and support of my parents, Achla and Om Prakash Jetley, and my children, Nirvana and Anshuman Bhatia. Special thanks also goes out to my Montessori sister, Dr. Martha M. Urioste, who saw the need for this story to be told my way. As I collected information for this book, I made so many friends all over the world who did everything they could to provide me with the knowledge I was seeking. I have acknowledged them in the chapters that follow, but want to say here that this book would not have been possible without them. Special mention must be made of Joke Verheul, Association Montessori Internationale, who has consistently and over the years been my first go to source. Finally, I would like to acknowledge the Montessori community – from Calcutta to Colorado – who have continuously inspired me for the past thirty years and some.

PREFACE

Like many other parents, I too was drawn to Montessori by my child. Pregnant and miles away from home, I knew a master's degree in English Literature was not going to help me raise a child. I wanted to do the best I could in my role as a mother and recognized there was no going back if I made a mistake. I consider myself very lucky that my path led me to Montessori. I embarked on the Montessori teacher-training course and am proud to say that both my children (adults now) are the result of a Montessori upbringing. Alongside raising them, I volunteered in their Montessori schools and later took on the roles of Montessori guide, teacher trainer, examiner, administrator, and consultant all over the world.

Through the thirty years and more that I have been involved in Montessori, I have studied Maria Montessori's philosophy and methodology in depth, reading her books over and over again, and each time coming up with something new. She never fails to surprise me, nudging me to think harder and deeper, and always making it clear that our work be centered on the child. She said in San Remo,

> "If we truly consider education to be the development of latent possibilities, rather than using the word education, we should adopt another: cultivation. The educator must cultivate the potentialities existing in the child, so they may develop and expand. It is essential to take advantage of this highly sensitive period in the life of the human being if, indeed, humanity is to improve" (1949, p. 6).

Not always do I see Dr. Montessori's practice reflected in schools that carry her name, and that saddens me to no end.

As the years go by, facts about her life are getting muddled; photographs are being incorrectly captioned and so many details are being lost and distorted. My journey in her footsteps began in 2006 when, for the first time, I visited the original Casa dei Bambini. This was almost like a pilgrimage for me and I wrote about it at that time (see Chapter 2). So much fell into place during the visit that I determined I would read her books again and try to visit other places of significance in her life. It helped me understand her better, as well as all the trials and tribulations she went through. I admired this woman even more (if that is possible) who never succumbed to challenges, and if she had to start all over again, she did so. She never gave up. It was all for the child, whether it be in Italy, Spain, England, the United States, or India. She was a pioneer and a remarkable educator who implemented methods through which young children learned social skills, spontaneous discipline, and achieved academic excellence unheard of until then. She said in San Remo,

> "I assure you that were I not absolutely certain that mankind can be bettered, I should not have had the strength to battle for fifty years, having so frequently had to begin again when my work was destroyed by others. I would not have had the strength, at my age, to travel the world, proclaiming the truth" (1949, p. 7).

Over the years, I have drawn so much strength from her life. She has given me a purpose, and I stay steadfast in my teacher's belief to do right by the child. I have my own little school now, Montessori Casa International in Denver, CO, in which I see on a daily basis the children happy and thriving as we cultivate their human spirit in the manner in which Maria Montessori guided us to do all those years ago, but still so relevant today. Between my teacher and the children in my school, I have led an inspired life, and I cannot thank Maria Montessori enough.

Revisiting Maria Montessori's Journey (1870-1952)

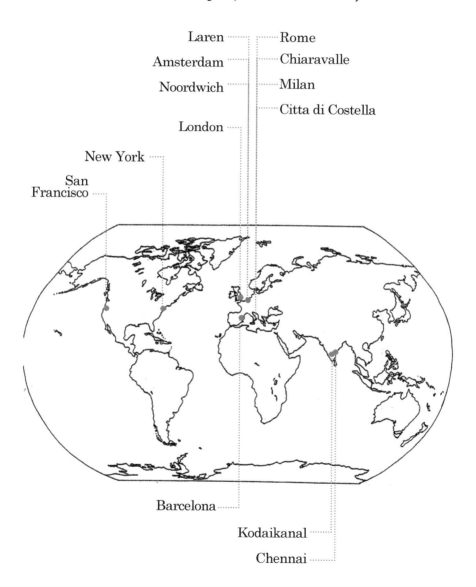

Laren ········ ········ Rome

Amsterdam ········ ····· Chiaravalle

Noordwich ········ ········ Milan

········ Citta di Costella

London ········

New York ········

San
Francisco ········

Barcelona ········

Kodaikanal ········

Chennai ········

FOREWORD

D r. Bhatia's "Cultivator of the Human Spirit: Revisiting Maria Montessori's Journey" is compelling, inspirational, and destined to encourage Montessorians to revisit Maria Montessori's journey on behalf of all children, educators, and parents in the 21st century. Our current educational system is in as much need of renovation as it was when Maria Montessori began her exploration of the cultivation of the human spirit. Maria Montessori's vision, mission, and life's work encompasses much more than simply the "The Montessori Method" and speaks to the need for a deeper philosophy that helps all children to reach their human potential in all facets of life.

It is my hope that upon reading this book each individual will be inspired with an increased desire, passion, and commitment to cultivate the child's human spirit. Dr. Bhatia's book includes captivating chapters of Dr. Montessori's history, stories, photos, and quotes. By visiting and doing on-site research in the many places that Dr. Montessori faced many challenges and victories during her lifetime, Dr. Bhatia is able to provide unique and important insight.

For me, the climax of the book was Dr. Bhatia's account of the tenacity required to find the "Rose Bank" bungalow where the Montessoris had lived. I could feel the trees where she was sitting and the flowers everywhere. Cosmic Education did emerge there and merits further contemplation. The final chapter takes the reader to Dr. Maria Montessori's final request on her tombstone...

"I ask the lovely children that can do everything to help me to build peace among people and in the world".

Let us continue to work with the children toward the day when there will be education that truly cultivates the individual spirit and peace in the world!

Martha M. Urioste, PhD
Denver Public School Educator
Montessori Elementary School Principal
Family Star Montessori School Co-Founder

Chapter 1
'La Dottoressa di Chiaravalle'

Maria Montessori's birthplace in Chiaravalle

M aria Tecla Artemisia Montessori was born on the 31st of August 1870 in Chiaravalle, Italy. This was the year when Prussia's attack on France forced Napoleon to withdraw his troops from the Papal States and Italy became united as a territory. However, there was still a long way to go and much work to be done before it could be united as a nation. Montessori's biographer, Rita Kramer writes:

> "...unification had changed the political format but hardly altered the social fabric in any radical way... local bureaucracy was only reinforced by a new superstructure of central regulations, and an essentially conservative monarchy was now in power" (1976, p. 19).

The new nation in which Maria Montessori was born was, in reality, very much like the old, traditional and conservative Italy.

Vast differences in wealth existed between the affluent and well educated who enjoyed immense power and privileges, and the poor, farm labor population. Traditionally, men went out to work and women took care of the home, and even though industrialization was bringing about a change, it was slow to break down the gender and social roles that were inherited across time and generations.

> "If family and class determined the status and careers of Italian males, women's roles were even more fixed by custom and tradition...women were expected to become the central sustaining force in their families as wives and mothers. With roles so determined, higher and professional education were not usually accessible to women" (Gutek, 2004, p. 2).

In contrast to the rest of Italy, Chiaravalle, a small hill town overlooking the Adriatic Sea, had a very different social climate. This was largely due to the presence of the tobacco industry which gave important impetus to the development of the Marche region. The Manifattura Tabacchi di Chiaravalle is one of the very first Italian industrial factories devoted to the cultivation and production of tobacco, whose foundation dates back to 1759. It was the engine of the transition from the agricultural economy to the industrial one, and saw the rise of the labor movement of women cigar makers and their social role, an example of feminine strength and working mothers.

The Cistercian monks, who came from France, started the tobacco industry in Chiaravalle. They worshipped the Virgin Mary and the female figure, and were very respectful of women. Tobacco grew in this area, and they created the tobacco factory especially to help women. Those who had nimble fingers were essential as they were needed to roll the cigars (later cigarettes). As a result, the women of this area began to earn more money than the men, many of who remained peasants. This changed the social dynamic tremendously. Women were powerful and strong, and the town had a feminist vibe. These smart women unionized when needed and demanded better working conditions for themselves. They combined their money and planted trees so they could walk to work in the shade. They created a daycare in their factory so their children could be taken care of while the women worked. They were very advanced, which put Chiaravalle way ahead of other towns in the Marche region. This was over a hundred years before Maria Montessori was born.

Maria Montessori was the daughter of Alessandro Montessori and Renilde Stoppani. Her father came from Ferrara (Northern Italy) and had a military upbringing. Kramer writes about him:

> " …was an old-fashioned gentleman of conservative temper and military habits. He had been a soldier in his youth, became a civil servant later in life, and belonged to a generation that welcomed the creation of the New Italy but found itself bewildered by many of the changes that came with it" (1976, p. 22).

4

Even though he came from a noble family, he had no money and, hence, like many others, he was attracted to the tobacco industry in Chiaravalle and decided to work there. Despite his role as an inspector and his involvement in quality control, he was working in a feminist environment and had to learn how to deal with powerful women. One of the women working there was Teckla Stoppani, who was the sister of Renilde Stoppani. Through Tecla, Alessandro met Renilde, who

> "...was unusually well educated for the time, a girl who devoured books in a town in which it was a matter of pride to be able to write one's name" (Kramer, 1976, p. 23).

They were married in the spring of 1866 and, as Kramer writes, made a very handsome couple, "the very image of respectability and prosperity" (1976, p. 23).

Chiaravalle Abbey

After a brief stay in Venice, the Montessoris returned to Chiaravalle and their only child, Maria Montessori, was born in Piazza Mazzini 10.

She was christened in the Chiaravalle Abbey which is right around the corner from her house. Chiaravalle Abbey is part of the Cistercian monastic complex and is a very striking structure. Dedicated to the Virgin Mary, it was built at the beginning of the twelfth century, combining two architectural styles: French Gothic and Lombard Romanesque.

Maria Montessori's biographer, E.M. Standing, noted that Montessori's strict childhood possibly influenced her educational method.

> "One day, on coming back from a month's holiday, little Maria began to complain: "I am hungry; I want something to eat." "You must wait a little while, dear," replied her mother. But the child would not wait, and became so insistent that her mother, opening a cupboard and finding

Chiaravalle Abbey where Maria Montessori was christened

Plaque by the City of Chiaravalle
honoring Dr. Montessori

a piece of bread left there from a month before, said, "If you cannot wait, take this!" (1957, p.22).

Maria's mother taught her daughter how to be compassionate by giving her the daily task of knitting for the poor. Maria herself chose to scrub a portion of the tile floor every day, and this perhaps was the beginning of the "exercises of practical life" that we find in all Montessori classrooms today.

She was very close to her aunt, Tecla, who continued to have a strong influence on her.

In 1876, Maria Montessori's father was transferred to Florence, and the family moved there for about eight months. They then finally settled in Rome. Montessori returned to Chiaravalle in 1950 when the Municipality honored her. Of this visit, she said, "Now I can finally die." A plaque outside her home honors this child of Chiaravalle.

The house is now open to visitors and students alike with original texts, photographs, and teaching materials. I was told during a visit there that Montessori very proudly autographed her photos and books as, "La Dottoressa di Chiaravalle/ The Doctor from Chiaravalle".

A strong foundation had been laid in Chiaravalle for an independent, determined woman and breaking conventional barriers became Montessori's norm. She initially aspired to be an engineer at a time when only two professions were open to women – nursing and teaching. Soon after she changed her mind and decided to enter medical school and become a doctor. Despite facing many obstacles due to her gender, Maria Montessori qualified as a doctor in July 1896. Soon after she was appointed

In Maria Montessori's bedroom which now exhibits original letters and books

Assistant Doctor at the Psychiatric Clinic in the University of Rome. This work initiated a deep interest in the needs of children with learning disabilities and Montessori studied the work of two early 19th century Frenchmen, Jean Itard and Eduoard Seguin. She was greatly influenced by their ideas and methods. From 1899 to 1901 she worked at the State Orthophrenic School where she developed and tested a variety of teaching materials. In 1901, she began her own studies of educational philosophy and anthropology, and in 1904, she was appointed a lecturer at the Pedagogic School of the University of Rome. The path was laid for "a crucial date: January 6th, 1907 – a decisive turning point that led to unexpected outcomes" (Trabalzini, 2011, p. 3).

Acknowledgements:
Francesco Mandolini, Fondazione Chiaravalle Montessori

Chapter 2
A diamond started to shine

"One entered under an archway. A wide walk went round the courtyard, and in the center bounded by a low green paling was a garden in which were little paths between grass and tall palms. The green of the palms against the white walls of the tenements produced a very striking effect. One turned to the right towards the Casa dei Bambini. The name was over the door. One entered and found oneself in a passage from which stairs led to the higher stories. A door on the right led into the antechamber in which the children on leaving hung the pinafores worn in school. The offices and the lavatory led from this antechamber, and another door opened into the working-room" (White, p. 63).

Today, as then, we still find the first "Children's House" situated on the ground floor of a residential building, and the approach to it is via a large atrium that leads to a courtyard and then to the school. This place has hardly changed since 1907 when the Casa dei Bambini first opened its doors to the fifty children.

> "with the object of preserving the property from the injuries done by the children below school age and of raising the standard of living of the inhabitants through the work done for the bambini" (p. 63).

A lot has changed, however, in the way the world views and knows the first Casa dei Bambini. My first visit here was in 2006 before the Centenary celebrations (2007) and the publicity this brought to the Casa in San Lorenzo. Smart phones and Google Maps have made a huge difference too in helping to locate the place. It was not so easy when I visited for the first time, and this is what I had written then:

[international]

Flowers for my Teacher...

Every summer my children and I enjoy exploring a different part of the world. Last summer we had settled on visiting the Eternal City – Rome. While I was naturally excited about appreciating the art and architecture, the cuisine and the scenery, I was equally enthusiastic about the prospect of visiting Montessori's first Casa dei Bambini. I consider myself a Montessorian (having been involved with the method for the past twenty years) but it was only when I made this pilgrimage to the Casa that every aspect of the method fell into place for me.

By Punum Bhatia

Standing in the archway to the courtyard cum playground

At only 36 years old, Maria Montessori was already recognized as a talented scientist, and was making grand discoveries in the academic world as she steadily created her own theories on child development. It was this growing reputation that caused a group of property developers to turn to her for an upcoming project which included renovating some of the city's older buildings. The project merely required a baby-sitter of sorts; as both mothers and fathers worked the entire day in the turn-of-the-century Roman slum neighborhood of San Lorenzo, their many children were left to run wild on the streets, defacing property as a result of their boredom, The city planners intended on Montessori keeping the children occupied in one area so that they would not have to repeatedly spend money in repainting the walls. She was thus given one large room and one helper, but no money for food or equipment.

"Casa dei Bambini" Inauguration Day: January 1907

On January 6, 1907, the first Casa dei Bambini opened and Montessori writes "that more than fifty children gathered together for the first time. It was interesting to note how different these little creatures were from those that usually attend preschools. They were in tears and seemed afraid of everything" (Montessori, 1967, p 35). As soon became evident, Montessori completely changed their lives, allowing them to not only find independence in their own lives, but also to better their entire community.

The Quartiere di San Lorenzo was not easy to find. Having finally decided on a general direction, the children and I began walking towards the large Termini Train Station. I was busy imagining what I would find at 58 Via di Marsi. I knew of no one who had been there before, and the only image I had came from a

Pigeons welcoming us to the San Lorenzo district

The first "Casa dei Bambini"

> I felt there should be some fanfare or fireworks going off. But there was nothing; this street too, was sparse. Had the school been in America, we would have been submerged in a mélange of souvenir shops, group tours, photo opportunities, and eating stalls.

photo snapped almost a century ago on the Inauguration day.

Crossing through the station we exited on the other side and turned right where a crumbling brick wall dictated our entrance into San Lorenzo.

Our only welcome to this district was a host of pigeons who flew off the left wall. The map and the road had come to an end. Should we turn right or left now?

Twists and turns

After many twists and turns, we eventually found Via di Marsi. Now, we just needed to find number 58 but the numbers seemed to be in no order. These were the streets on which the children played, the buildings they had burdened with graffiti; this was where Montessori gathered her first students and subsequently changed the course of child psychology.

A bronze plaque caught the sunlight and within all the Italian, I recognized the word 'Montessori'. Directly above the plaque was a square tile with the numerals 5 and 8 painted on it.

I felt there should be some fanfare or fireworks going off. But there was nothing; this street too, was sparse. Had the school been in America, we would have been submerged in a mélange of souvenir shops, group tours, photo opportunities, and food stalls. Yet this place managed to retain the simplicity and individuality that Montessori had discovered a hundred years ago. An

arched foyer greeted us before we moved into the expansive courtyard bathed in light.

Four large yellow buildings surrounded a green courtyard laden with dusty-blue hydrangea flowers. The building to our immediate right bore the title "Maria Montessori, Casa dei Bambini".

The irony was that someone had left their blue bathrobe and other articles of laundry to dangle over the brass letters. So many years ago, Montessori had pioneered a method here that allowed the children to have pride in themselves and their surroundings, causing them to forbid their mothers from hanging the laundry outside but encouraging them to put out window boxes of geraniums and other flowers,

I was overcome with emotion; suddenly, everything that I had read and taught over the years fell into place as I devoured the environment in which the method had been cultivated.

I thought about Montessori being here, observing the children at work, and changing the materials as she deemed necessary, the method evolving all the time.

As I climbed the stairs to enter the apartment building, (the school was simply one of the apartments on the ground floor), I pictured Montessori here and the children welcoming her in the morning. This was where she took the four-month old baby from her mother in the courtyard to show the children, —

the origin of the Silence Game.

The school was closed for the summer of course, so we could not enter the actual classroom. A feeling of gratitude enveloped me and I made a silent promise to spread her ideals as faithfully and truly as I possibly could.

There was a brass handle on the brown door and on that I placed a bunch of that abundant dusty blue hydrangea. I had not thought twice about doing so; it was an instinctive gesture. In India, we always take flowers to our 'guru.'

The Casa dei Bambini still functions as a Public Montessori preschool in the San Lorenzo district of Rome. There are two classrooms with about 25 children in each. Each classroom has one teacher trained in the Montessori method by the Opera Nazionale Montessori. The school runs from 8.30am to 4.30pm. An International Congress is being planned for January 2007 to celebrate its centenary. ■

Punum Bhatia is a Director and Teacher Educator at Montessori Center International (MCI), Denver, USA.

Bibliography:

Kramer, R (1988), *Maria Montessori, A Biography,* Addison-Wesley Publishing Company Inc.

Montessori, M (1986), *The Secret of Childhood* Orient Longman, 1986

Montessori, M (1967), *The Discovery of the Child,* Ballantine Books, New York

Maria Montessori writes:

> "It was near the end of the year 1906...A great
> opportunity came to me, for I was invited by Edoardo
> Talamo, the Director General of the Roman Association
> for Good Building, to undertake the organization of
> infant schools in its model tenements. It was Signor
> Talamo's happy idea to gather together in a large room
> all the little ones between the ages of three and seven
> belonging to the families living in the tenement. The
> play and work of these children was to be carried on
> under the guidance of a teacher who should have her
> own apartment in the tenement house" (2004, p. 89).

In the late nineteenth century, Rome faced many social
problems that came as a result of rapidly doubling its population
and becoming a modern city. Immigrants came from the
countryside looking for a better life, and entrepreneurs took
advantage of the need for more housing by going into a construction
frenzy. New apartments came up all over the city, but it was growth
that came too fast and enterprises began to fail and crash.

One such project stood in the San Lorenzo ward of Rome,
situated between the Aurelian walls, the University, and the
historical cemetery of Campo Verano. It did not meet the needs
and demands of the working class population, and hence it was
abandoned. However, this was not for long. As Montessori's
biographer, Rita Kramer writes,

> "Beggars and criminals found it a convenient shelter and
> hiding place. Thousands of the homeless poor crowded
> in, and the police were reluctant to penetrate what were
> described as "these grim walls of crime and horror." With
> no sanitation and no policing, it became a hellhole of
> infection and prostitution, an abode of the dead as well
> as the living... The press referred to the Quartiere di San
> Lorenzo as "the shame of Italy" (1976, p. 109).

The archway leading to the Casa dei Bambini

Casa dei Bambini, 58 Via dei Marsi, San Lorenzo

The *Istituto Romano dei Beni Stabili* (Roman Real Estate Institute) under the director of its engineer, Edoardo Talamo, aimed at reclaiming the existing buildings and constructing new ones. The apartment building situated at 58 Via dei Marsi was one of their first projects. They aimed at bringing about a moral change in the inhabitants of the buildings, wanting them to cooperate and be responsible for the upkeep of the common spaces. However, during the day when the parents went out to work, the children, too young for school, ran

> "wild throughout the building, defacing the newly whitewashed walls and using their ingenuity on whatever other petty acts of vandalism they could invent. Something had to be done with them to protect the investment of the builders, and the directors decided the most effective solution would probably be to gather them together in one place and keep them occupied there all day" (Kramer, 1976, p. 110).

Plaque dedicated to Talamo in the original Casa dei Bambini

Talamo asked Maria Montessori, already known as a university lecturer and committed to working with children and women, to manage the organization of the school. Despite their later misunderstandings regarding discipline issues and their fallout, Montessori always remembered Talamo as the promoter of the Children's Houses. To this day, a plaque in the original Casa dei Bambini honors him.

For Maria Montessori, this was an opportunity to try out some of her educational ideas on typically developing children. She was given nothing but a bare room and a supervising adult with fifty children to occupy. "It would have seemed preposterous to anyone-with the possible exception of Montessori herself-that what went on in that room would become known all over Italy within a year and all over the world within five more" (Kramer, 1976, p. 111).

16

On January 6th, 1907, the first Casa dei Bambini opened at 58 Via dei Marsi with a formal inauguration ceremony. Montessori describes the entrance of the children:

> "They were dressed all alike in some thick, heavy blue drill. They were frightened and being hindered by the stiff material, could move neither arms nor legs freely. Apart from their own community they had never seen any people. To get them to move together, they were made to hold hands. The first unwilling child was pulled, thus dragging along the whole line of the rest. All of them were crying miserably" (1970, p. 4).

Later, Montessori confessed that during that very morning, standing before 50 crying and frightened children, that she had the indefinable feeling that made her announce that a great work was beginning:

> "From the very first I perceived, in all its immensity, the social and pedagogical importance of such institutions, and while at that time my visions of a triumphant future seemed exaggerated, today many are beginning to understand that what I saw before was indeed the truth" (Montessori, 2004, p. 89).

One of the first Children's Houses in San Lorenzo

This first Casa dei Bambini was very different from the Montessori classrooms we know today. Kramer mentions that the furniture in the room consisted of tables on which three children sat alongside each other, a teacher's desk, and a storage cabinet in which toys and materials were locked up. Jessie White, who visited the school in 1913, writes:

> "This attendant took the material out of the cupboard and passed it round. The directrice told the children not to talk while it was being given out. The children, however, had some choice as to what they took. They shared between them the various frames, the solid and plane insets, the broad stair, the long stair, and some of the sandpaper letters" (p. 65).

The children were left in the care of Candida Nuccitelli, who worked under the guidance and direction of Maria Montessori and lived in the same apartment complex as the school. Montessori herself would visit the Casa whenever she could, bringing with her modified Itard and Seguin materials, and would observe the children working with them. She would tell Candida to make the materials available to the children, with no restrictions or specifications.

> "I merely wanted to study the children's reactions. I asked her not to interfere with them in any way as otherwise I would not be able to observe them" (Montessori, 1970, p. 5).

Within a few weeks, Montessori noticed changes in the children:

> "From timid and wild as they were before, the children became sociable and communicative. They showed different relationships with each other. Their personalities grew and they showed extraordinary understanding, activity, vivacity and confidence. They were happy and joyous" (1970, p. 5).

With the respect they had been given and the opportunities to choose their own tasks, the children showed unmatched capabilities to concentrate and work. She watched with fascination the intentness of a three-year-old girl working with knobbed cylinders, taking them out, mixing them up, and replacing them over and over again. She writes in "The Secret of Childhood":

> "I then decided to see how concentrated she was in her strange employment. I told the teacher to have the other children sing. But this did not disturb the child at all in her labors. I then gently picked up the chair in which she was sitting and set it on top of a

Child working on Knobbed Cylinders, Princess Elizabeth Montessori School, Edinburgh

small table. As I lifted the chair she clutched the objects with which she was working and placed them on her knees, but then continued with the same task. From the time I began to count, she repeated the exercise forty-two times. Then she stopped as if coming out of a dream and smiled happily. Her eyes shone brightly and she looked about. She had not even noticed what we had done to disturb her. And now, for no apparent reason, her task was finished" (1966, p. 119).

As a result of her observations, Montessori began to change

the furniture to low cupboards and washbasins, light tables that could be easily moved by the children, and blackboards on the wall. Above the blackboards, there hung a copy of Raphael's "Madonna della Seggiola", which Montessori chose as the emblem of the Children's Houses and which still hangs in the school today.

Madonna della Seggiola hangs on the walls of the original Casa die Bambini

"A diamond started to shine." (Trabalzini, 2011, p. 53) in the streets of San Lorenzo and they began to receive lots of visitors.

> "More and more people wanted to see the diamond shining within the walls of the Children's House, and visitors came in large numbers: as the journalist and writer Sofia Bisi Albini commented, "there is no person interested in social and educational issues who, coming to Rome, does not visit the model homes of the Societa dei Beni Stabili and its Children's Houses – and visiting and admiring them is all one and the same. I saw ladies who would not normally be put out by any idea, become real propagandists of the new method of child education" (Trabalzini, 2011, p. 56-57).

Foyer of the original Casa dei Bambini which leads to the classroom

The first Casa dei Bambini continues to operate as a Montessori school, after a brief closure soon after World War II and 1966, when it was reopened on the initiative of the Rome section of Opera Montessori. It is an inspiration for those of us connected with Montessori and I, for one, can never visit often enough.

"More and more people wanted to see the diamond shining" (Trabalzini, 2011, p. 56) and a second Casa dei Bambini opened four months later.

Acknowledgements:
Manola Daga, Casa dei Bambini San Lorenzo

Chapter 3
"I can write! I can write!"

Children writing on the floor of the terrace of the second Casa dei Bambini

On April 7th, 1907, just three months after the opening of the first Casa dei Bambini, a second Children's House opened in the San Lorenzo district. In view of the good results achieved, the rooms situated on the ground floor of another building within the same apartment complex were put to the same use. These rooms could also be accessed from Via dei Campani 55. In her inaugural address, Maria Montessori said:

> "This is not simply a place where the children are kept, not just an asylum, but a true school for their education... We see here for the first time the possibility of realizing the long-talked-of pedagogical idea. We have put the school within the home; and this is not all. We have placed it within the home as the property of the community, leaving under the eyes of the parents the whole life of the teacher in the accomplishment of her mission.
>
> This idea of the community ownership of the school is new and very beautiful and profoundly educational.
>
> The parents know that the Casa dei Bambini is their property, and is maintained by a portion of the rent they pay. The mothers may go any hour of the day to watch..." (Kramer, 1976, p. 123).

There is no mention here of her didactic method; only that the Children's House would not be a passive shelter but a real house of education.

Montessori saw the Casa dei Bambini as a social institution – with a home-school link and the socialization of the modern home. She called for the cooperation between the family and the school, believing it was an essential need of educational activities. The Children's Houses had a dual educational role: educating the children and also educating their parents. Since women were obliged to work away from home, the structure of the family changed and Montessori placed her Children's Houses within this background of the family's structure in the modern world. As is obvious from her inaugural address, the social function of the new institution excited her. The working mothers could leave their children at the Casa "with a feeling of great relief and freedom to their own work". But this benefit, like that of the care of the house, is not conferred without a tax of care and good will. The regulations posted on the walls announced this: "the mothers are obliged to send their children to the 'Children's House' clean, and to co-operate with the Directress in the educational work" (Montessori, 2004, p. 99). The parents had a responsibility to fulfill, looking after the physical and moral care of their own children and, if at any time it was considered that the work of the school was being undermined by the attitude at home, the child was sent home.

> "In other words, the parents must learn to deserve the benefit of having within the house the great advantage of a school for their little ones" (Montessori, 2004, p. 99).

Montessori concluded her inaugural address by speaking of the "new woman" and "new man", united in the socialized home, which was a "true and worthy nest for human couples who, within it, wish to improve the species and launch it in the eternity of life" (Trabalzini, 2011, p. 51).

The classroom of the second Casa

I was excited to visit the second Casa, particularly because this is where that first explosion into writing described by Montessori took place. It was a smaller room than the first Casa with windows that overlooked the playground and the garden. Rita Kramer writes about the transformation of the children,

> "Again at this second Casa, Montessori chose an untrained-therefore, from her point of few, unspoiled-young woman as directress, and again the children who came on the first day disorganized, bewildered, and often sullen immediately showed a spontaneous interest in handling the materials, gradually worked their way from the simpler to the more complicated ones on their own, and soon became cheerful and responsible as well as strikingly competent at their tasks" (1976, p. 125).

The curriculum consisted mostly of the Exercises of Practical Life and Education of the Senses. "I had not," Montessori wrote, "presented exercises for writing, because, like everybody else, I held the prejudice that it was necessary to begin as late as possible the teaching of reading and writing, and certainly to avoid it before the age of six" (2004, p. 201). It was on the children's persistence and the insistence of the mothers who came to Montessori and asked that she teach their children to read and write that she decided to give it a try when the school reopened in September. It was in December that the explosion into writing took place. Montessori recollects:

> "I went up on the roof with the children. They were playing freely about, and a number of them were gathered around me. I was sitting near a chimney, and said to a little five-year-old boy who sat beside me, 'Draw me a picture of this chimney,' giving him as I spoke a piece of chalk. He got down obediently and made a rough sketch of the chimney on the tiles which formed the floor of this roof terrace. As is

The garden at the second Casa

my custom with little children, I encouraged him, praising his work. The child looked at me, smiled, remained for a moment as if on the point of bursting into some joyous act, and then cried out, 'I can write! I can write!' and kneeling down again he wrote on the pavement the word 'hand'. Then, full of enthusiasm, he wrote also 'chimney', 'roof'. As he wrote, he continued to cry out, 'I can write! I know how to write!'" (2004, p. 213-214).

Soon after, other children began to write, too. None had written before, and when they did, it was not a letter or two but the whole word. Montessori continues to describe the excited children writing everywhere – blackboard, overturned chairs, window shutters, doors, whatever they could find! It was all here in the second Casa dei Bambini.

Jessie White, who visited this Casa in 1913 and observed the children, wrote:

> "It was interesting to watch them at work. They showed remarkable power of self-criticism. The little girl with the bows undid the second bow repeatedly as though she could not satisfy herself. Similarly, when the children were writing on the slates, they rubbed out a letter several times before the shape was perfect enough to please them. Excellence rather than quantity seemed the motive of their action" (1913, p. 85).

It is no wonder that the Montessori movement began to capture international attention "and the four and five year olds who learned to write in less than two months and to read in a matter of days after that astonished the world" (Kramer, 1976, p. 13).

Tucked away in the corner of the two Casa dei Bambinis is a garden of which Maria Montessori writes:

> "we have a courtyard, cultivated as a garden, where the children are free to run in the open air – and, besides, a long stretch of ground, which is planted on one side with trees, has a branching path in the middle, and on the opposite side, has broken ground for the cultivation of plants. The last, we have divided into so many portions, reserving one for each child" (2004, p. 147).

These gardens exist to this day with many fruit trees: plum, pomegranate, apple, lemon, apricot, to mention a few. There are

Pomegranate

Apple

jasmine creepers, bamboo, strawberries, and grape vines as well.
Montessori goes on to describe the garden project at San Lorenzo:

> "While the smaller children run freely up and down the
> paths, or rest in the shade of the trees, the possessors of
> the earth (children from four years of age), are sowing,
> or hoeing, watering or examining, the surface of the soil
> watching for the sprouting of the plants" (2004, p. 147).

What touched me most about this garden was the rose bush
in the corner. It was in full bloom and attracted me so much that
I had to walk toward it. The smell was powerful, and as I fingered
the roses, I was told that Maria Montessori herself planted this
bush. They went on to tell me that an ex-student of the Casa who
had been there when Maria Montessori used to visit it had told
them that it was from this place where the rose bush stands that
Montessori liked to observe the children.

Just as the children of the first Casa dei Bambini brought a
change in the residents of the building by getting them to stop

Rose bush in the second Casa planted by Maria Montessori

hanging their wash out of the windows and replacing it with
flower boxes instead, a change came about in the gardens of San
Lorenzo, too. Maria Montessori wrote:

> "the little reservations of the children are placed along the
> wall of the tenement, in a spot formerly neglected because
> it leads to a blind road; the inhabitants of the house,
> therefore, had the habit of throwing from those windows
> every kind of offal, and at the beginning our garden was
> thus contaminated.

But, little by little, without any exhortation on our part, solely through the respect born in the people's mind for the children's labor, nothing more fell from the windows, except the loving glances and smiles of the mothers upon the soil which was the beloved possession of their little children" (2004, p. 147).

The Second Casa dei Bambini, like the first, and the adjoining gardens operated under the management of the Istituto Romano dei Ben Stabili until 1933 when it was donated to the Roman government. They continued to operate until the first years after the Second World War, after which they fell into complete disuse. Only in 1969 was the Children's House in Via dei Campani 55 reopened, and in 1976 it became a State school. It continues to operate as a separate branch of the VII Maria Montessori School District.

By the fall of 1907, Montessori began to experiment with teaching materials for reading and writing (sandpaper letters and the large movable alphabet box) and this attracted further public attention to her work. She was invited by the Umanitaria Society to enter into a partnership and open more schools in Milan.

Acknowledgments:
Tiziana Bertini and Ilaria Valentini, Casa dei Bambini San Lorenzo

Vines provide a beautiful shade cover in the garden of the second Casa

Chapter 4
"Deeply grateful..."
Maria Montessori in Milan

Casa dei Bambini in Umanitaria (1936)
(Societa Umanitaria Archives, Milan)

In 1907, Dr. Maria Montessori's revolutionary experiment with the children in San Lorenzo, Rome, had caught the attention of people all over the world. "This experiment which had had its beginnings in a landlord's desire to keep the children from scribbling on the walls had had a somewhat unexpected result: they had learned to write on them" (Kramer, 1976, p. 130). Only a year had passed since successfully starting the pedagogical practice in the San Lorenzo neighborhood when Maria Montessori received and accepted an invitation to create a similar facility in Milan.

It was on July 1, 1908 that the Umanitaria Board decided to create a House of Children in the social housing estate in via Solari, Milan, for children between the ages of three and six years. "Founded by Jewish socialists, Umanitaria was a center for working-class families that provided modern housing and such social services as occupational training in model workshops, employment referral, and adult education facilities" (Kramer, 1976, p. 135). Built in only a year (between April 1905 and March 1906), the social housing estate for workers located in via Solari soon became one of the best examples of social housing in Italy. The Umanitaria had responded quickly to an urgent need of the times, steering away from its original purpose. The 280,000 working class people had no choice but to live in houses with no ventilation or lighting. Having acknowledged the problem, the Umanitaria allocated a large sum of money for the construction of a workers' housing estate which would meet social standards.

In a meeting with the personnel of the Umanitaria, the houses were described to me as "equipped with private toilets, garbage disposals, kitchen sinks, drinking water, and electricity". Designed by Giovanni Broglio, there were 249 apartments in this social housing experiment that were also given additional services and activities. These included a library and the Casa dei Bambini, which earned the Umanitaria Estate the title of Pioneer of Social Housing.

Societa Umanitaria Milan

It was Augusto Osimo, the Secretary of the Umanitaria Society, who was responsible for fostering a highly successful partnership with Maria Montessori. Montessori, who had been involved in the Women's Right movement soon after her medical career began and was in touch with the milieu of Milan feminists for years, viewed the spirit and self-governing practices embodied by the Umanitaria as a promising breeding ground for implementing her pedagogical practice. She was known for her high levels of competency in treating patients, but also for the respect she showed to patients from all classes. The notion of social reform became a strong theme throughout her life. She focused on developing independence since early childhood with the hope that this would improve mankind as a whole. The Umanitaria's readiness to pioneer cutting-edge initiatives convinced her that it would be the ideal host for the experimentation of her method.

Invitation to the inauguration of the Casa dei Bambini (1908)
(Societa Umanitaria Archives, Milan)

Inauguration Day of the First Montessori School in Milan (1908)
(Societa Umanitaria Archives, Milan)

Simultaneously, the carpenters at the Casa di Lavoro (The House of Labor) undertook the manufacturing of the teaching apparatus for the school. Alessandrina Ravizza, who shared Montessori's commitment to women's emancipation, was in charge of this endeavor. The Casa di Lavoro remained for a long time the principal producer and supplier of Montessori materials, both nationally and internationally. The Casa dei Bambini in via Solari opened on October 18th, 1908.

> "It was the beginning of a longstanding relationship between Montessori and Umanitaria, which over the years was to establish other Montessori schools and sponsor teacher-training courses, conferences, and exhibitions of the didactic materials" (Kramer, 1976, p. 135).

After a very rewarding time spent at the Umanitaria, where I was privy to the Montessori archives and had many of my questions answered, I made my way to the site of the third Casa. All I had in my hand was a piece of paper on which was written "via Solari 40"; but thanks to the taxi driver, it was not a problem at all to find this apartment complex. While I asked the driver to wait, I walked in and must have looked completely lost and out of place because a young lady came up to me and asked what I was there for! When I explained, she told me I was walking the wrong way and directed me to turn around. She stayed with me as we walked together, and in the meanwhile she called a very knowledgeable gentleman whom she said knew much more than she did. He joined us within minutes! I was flattered and honored with the attention I was getting, but also so excited to be there. At once, this reminded me of the first Casa dei Bambini in San Lorenzo, Rome. It was the same idea of a school within an apartment complex. Anna M. Maccheroni, who was in charge of the school, described it as such:

> "Our premises consisted of a large room containing all the little tables and chairs and a big cupboard with glass doors in which was all the material. Off this was a small room in which was my piano. There was a bathroom and three W.C's. We had also a small garden, in the center of which was a basin in which were several goldfish; in a recess was a little hen house with a hen-run" (1947, p. 19).

Casa Bambini via Lombardia (1910)
(Societa Umanitaria Archives, Milan)

With Maccheroni's detailed description, I could see it all so clearly as I stood outside the third Casa.

There were forty-six children in the school, all under the age of six.

The Casa dei Bamnin at via Solari then (1908) and now (2018)
(Societa Umanitaria Archives, Milan)

To assist Anna Maccheroni was Clementina, who cleaned the school and helped a little with the children. Maccheroni writes,

> "This was the first experiment outside of Rome, and I felt the responsibility. It was arranged that for the first two months no visitors should be admitted. At the end of this period the children had acquired self-discipline" (1947, p. 20).

It took them only two months to be self-disciplined! Maccheroni describes incidents of taking the children for a walk alongside a canal and warning them not to get too close to the edge for fear of falling into the water.

> "These children were not used to being taken out for a walk; many of them had never even been taken into town... They threw in small branches, and watched them being carried away by the current. This incident proved to me

that they had attained self-control. In the early days they could not even cross the threshold to the garden without pushing and tumbling over one another" (1947, p. 20-21).

Jessie White, who visited the school in 1913, writes:

"During the time I spent in the Via Solari I never saw any child whose will came into conflict with that of the directrice. The relations between the adults and children were entirely trustful and loving... The atmosphere was one of real courtesy, and the directrice in the Via Solari could be her natural self, cheerful, alert, composed, and enjoying the children as one can only enjoy them when they are free to reveal themselves, and when one is conscious that one need not drag them to a certain level of achievement to meet the requirements of others, whether it is good for them to be so dragged or not" (1914, p. 41).

In response to a letter from Augusto Osimo conveying gratitude for including the Umanitaria in the Casa dei Bambini experiment and hoping for continuing collaboration, Maria Montessori responded,

"It is not you who should thank me, but I who should be deeply grateful to all those who have honored the work to which I am devoted by entrusting it to the Societa Umanitaria, which will be able to perfect, spread and develop it as a means of raising the people".

Montessori saw this partnership as an opportunity to quickly spread what she had started in San Lorenzo.

It was not long after that the success of the first experiment with the Housing Estate for Workers in via Solari that the Umanitaria was encouraged to repeat its efforts. The second Housing Estate for Workers opened in the northeastern suburbs of the city and was an improvement to the first. According to the personnel of the Umanitaria that I met, there were 214 apartments

Casa Bambini via Lombardia (1913)
(Societa Umanitaria Archives, Milan)

built between October 1908 and November 1909, and these apartments had "larger rooms with better services such as electricity, toilets, heating and a higher focus on privacy". The estate also included a Casa dei Bambini and community facilities such as large courtyards, shops, recreation clubs, and libraries.

The second Casa dei Bambini in Milan opened on November 21st, 1909, with Anna Fedeli as the Directress.

When I arrived at Viale Lombardia, I was struck with how similar it was to via Solari.

There were two ladies in the front courtyard chatting with each other while keeping an eye on a small child. When they looked my way, I used the little bit of Italian I had picked up and explained why I was there. I was told the building was "abandoned" a few years ago. Nevertheless, I told them I would like to see where it was. I am not quite sure what they made of me, but they took me to it right away! The gate was locked, so I peered in as much as I could, walking all around and taking as many photos as I could.

Casa Bambini via Lombardia now (2018)

Mussolini in Umanitaria (1934)
(Societa Umanitaria Archives, Milan)

What caught my attention was a sink in the playground, at child's height, and I wondered what stories it could tell.

Jessie White writes of her visit to this Montessori school in 1913:

> "One feature in which this Casa differed from the other was in the greater frequency with which the parents came into the school. Some mothers were constantly in and out, and a visitor had the opportunity of seeing the happy relations, which existed between them and the directrice. They seemed to feel for her the same devotion that was felt by the children and to come under the influence of her kindly, gentle tranquility" (194, p. 46).

In 1914, the third Casa dei Bambini in Milan was opened in the Umanitaria itself. Maria Montessori insisted with Augusta Osimo that there be at least one school – even a small one – where the Method was applied well and correctly. So it was at the headquarters of the Umanitaria (in via San Barnaba) that a model school was opened.

Unfortunately, it was destroyed during World War II and there was nothing I could see, except for a photo or two of Mussolini visiting the school in 1934.

The social housing experiment developed by the Umanitaria, of which the Casa dei Bambini was an integral part, became an internationally respected model for its pioneering approach, original concept, and generous facilities. The collaboration between the Umanitaria and Maria Montessori continued with the organization of training courses for teachers, lectures, and the publication of "La Coltura Popolare" with articles by Montessori and others, as well as reports on the spread of Montessori schools worldwide. In the following years, this magazine became one of the fundamental means of dissemination of the new pedagogy, playing a role of primary importance in the transmission of the thought and work of Maria Montessori.

News of Montessori's approach spread rapidly and visitors came to see for themselves how she was achieving such amazing results with the children. Among those that came were Baroness Alice Hallgarten and Baron Leopoldo Franchetti who believed so strongly in Montessori's work that they invited her to their home in Citta di Castello.

Acknowledgements:
Claudio Colombo, Societa Umanitaria Milan

Casa dei Bambini via Solari (1912)
(Societa Umanitaria Archives, Milan)

(Societa Umanitaria Archives, Milan)

Chapter 5
The Summer of 1909: Citta di Castello

Villa Montesca, Citta di Castello

The San Lorenzo experiment was such a success that visitors came in large numbers to see it. These visitors included Baron Leopoldo Franchetti and Baroness Alice Hallgarten. Leopoldo Franchetti was an Italian politician and economist who was interested in the problems of the rural people and focused his work on agricultural economic reforms in Southern Italy. His report in *La Sicilia nel 1876* described the life of the farmers as the hardest in all of Italy and he directed his efforts toward the improvement of both their life and conditions. His wife, Alice Hallgarten, was passionate about education and believed that the way to improve the social conditions of the farmers was through a change in the educational system. She opened schools in their Villa Montesca and Rovigliano for the education of the children of farm workers.

In 1909, Franchetti and Hallgarten visited the Casa dei Bambini in San Lorenzo and were highly impressed by Dr. Maria

Baron Leopoldo Franchetti and Baroness Alice Hallgarten (Archives of Hallgarten-Franchetti Foundation Città di Castello)

The terrace of Villa Montesca

Montessori's work and new approach to education. They believed this had "an importance for the whole humanity" and invited her to spend some time at Villa Montesca to train the teachers of the rural school they had opened, as well as put her methodology in writing. "These words and this method must not wander from mouth to mouth, but must become a means of propaganda" (Trabalzini, 2011, p. 56). It was an immediate call to action.

> "It is your duty", insisted Baron Franchetti, with whose family she was staying as a guest in the summer of 1909. "You might suddenly die; and then nothing of it would remain." Montessori herself was rather amused at this, because, as she says, "I was in excellent health at the time" (Standing, 1957, p. 57).

Montessori accepted the invitation and came to Villa Montesca near the town of Citta di Castello (in Umbria). Anna Maccheroni wrote of this time:

> "How well I remember the joy of that summer at the villa, the lovely hills all around! On a spacious "terrazza" Baronessa had a curious instrument so made that, when the wind blew, a sweet sound was heard, "the voice of the wind" (1947, p. 29).

During my visit to Villa Montesca, I was told that Montessori and Hallgarten would meet in the terrace, overlooking the beautiful hills, every evening to discuss the events of the day.

It was there, in the library and in the lovely green park, that Maria Montessori "found the right conditions for a piece of work that would carry her name around the world" (Kramer, 1976, p. 137). It took her only twenty days for the manuscript for *Il Metodo della Pedagogia Scientifica*, in which she describes her San Lorenzo experience, to be ready. This later appeared as *The Montessori Method*. The Franchetti's arranged for the publication of the book, sending it directly to the printing house to avoid anything being changed. Maria Montessori dedicated it:

Corsa di Pedagogia Scientifica publication (1909)

> "To the noblewoman Baroness Alice Franchetti Hallgarten and to Baron Leopoldo Franchetti, Senator of the Kingdom,

In the Library where 'The Montessori Method' was written

I dedicate this book which they wanted and thanks to them comes out today to the life of thought, baptizing in scientific literature the 'Children's Houses'" (Trabalzini, 2011, p. 59).

The Franchetti's were excellent hosts and took good care of Maria Montessori. Anna Maccheroni wrote:

> "Baronessa, generous and kind-hearted, took great care that Dr. Montessori should rest. Sometimes she took all books from her room, put the room in black darkness, and said, "Now you will be able to have a good rest!" (1947, p. 29).

Maria Montessori also enjoyed spending time outside in the open green park and had a favorite tree under which she would rest. This tree is very much alive today and among the most interesting I have seen.

Following the publication of the book, in August 1909, Dr.

Montessori's favorite tree at Villa Montesca

Montessori gave her first training, *Course of scientific pedagogy*, to teachers from Italy. Anna Maccheroni mentions that there were about one hundred students who attended, most of them were teachers.

> "The teachers seemed to accept the Montessori idea with great interest and hope...It was of great interest to see teachers, some of them no longer young, enter into the new idea with a feeling of warm content. How much they understood, how deeply they went into it, it would be difficult to say, but surely there was a spiritual stimulus in these lectures; the child was considered from a point of view so different from what was – at that time – to be found in books for teachers, that the students felt as if they were breathing bracing air" (Maccheroni, 1947, p. 28).

Each of the students received a copy of the new book, and the course ended with an awarding of diplomas ceremony at the villa.

With the success of the book and the first training course, "everything changes: interviews, conferences, invitations abroad, the Doctor is now launched" (Cavini, 2013). She was always grateful to the Franchetti's saying,

> "I was left in the dark, without help, no one to lift me, to support me in this human labour...Many visited the Children's House to restore themselves in the spiritual bath, but only the Baroness Franchetti understood that this water would invigorate humanity" (Cavini, 2013).

Later, when the first English edition of *Il Metodo della Pedagogia Scientifica applicator all' educazione infantile nelle Casa Dei Bambini* was published under the title of *The Montessori Method*, Dr. Montessori recognized the role of Alice Franchetti in making it possible.

The Montessori School in Villa Montesca (1909)
(Archives of Hallgarten-Franchetti Foundation Città di Castello)_

The classroom in the Tella Umbra Museum

Old Montessori materials in the Tella Umbra Museum

Together, they opened Montessori schools in Villa Montesca and Rovigliano, as well as in the linen factory (Tella Umbra) of

Alice Franchetti for the children of unwed mothers who worked there.

The educational materials used in the schools as well as the old school desks and inkwells can be found in the Tella Umbra Museum. The summer of 1909 ended with Montessori and her companions traveling to Perugia; and then in the fall, Montessori returned to Rome, planning for future training courses.

The participants of the first Montessori training course in Villa Montesca, Citta di Castello (Archives of Hallgarten-Franchetti Foundation Città di Castello)

Maria Montessori in Citta di Castello with Alice
Hallgarten (Archives of Hallgarten-Franchetti
Foundation Città di Castello)

Acknowledgments:
Fabrizio Boldrini, Paola Angelini, Manfredi Treggiam and
Marco Conti, Citta di Castello

Chapter 6
New Experimental Science: Rome

Montessori's home in Rome (1913)

By 1910, Maria Montessori was no longer involved in the schools in San Lorenzo. Due to a disagreement with Signor Talamo, she was not even allowed to visit the school. Rita Kramer explains:

> "Years later, it was revealed that the "disagreement" resulted from Talamo's resentment of the publicity which centered on Montessori's educational experiment rather than, as he had hoped, on his housing experiment in which it took place" (1976, p. 146).

However, Montessori stayed positive and saw these closed doors as "providential. They always make for progress" (Kramer, 1976, p. 146).

She was now living with her parents at Via Principessa Clothilde in Rome. The apartment had a large balcony with a great view of the Piazzo del Popolo and the Pincian Hills. Montessori loved taking walks in Pincio Park, and it was here,

Piazzo del Popolo, Rome

many years earlier, that she found her purpose in life. E.M. Standing writes about the struggles of the young doctor who reached a breaking point and left the dissecting room in despair:

> "It happened that her way home led through the Pincio Park, which at that hour was almost empty of people. As she walked along, thinking of her decision, she passed a shabbily dressed woman accompanied by a child of some two years of age...It was not the woman, however, but the child who was destined to alter the course of her life" (1957, p. 25).

She watched him play with a small piece of colored paper and was so moved by the child's expression - "so serenely happy in the possession of that worthless scrap of colored paper, observing it with the full absorption of its little soul" (Standing, 1957, p. 25) that she immediately turned around and went back to the dissecting room. She never looked back for now she knew she had a vocation.

It was in the Villa Borghese gardens (Pincio Park is on its western edge) too that Montessori met Queen Margherita for the first time. The medical students had organized a festival of flowers and the guests came in carriages decorated with many different kinds of flowers. Among them was Queen Margherita who won first prize.

> "The honor of presenting the award of a hand-painted banner and a bouquet to her majesty was given to the attractive young female student of medicine, Maria Montessori. In her first recorded public appearance, Montessori exhibited both tact and persistence. The queen demurred; she did not wish to accept the prize, she asked that it be given to someone else. Montessori found the right words to convince the queen who, at Maria's gentle insistence found herself graciously

accepting the prize from the hands of the young student" (Kramer, 1976, p. 46-47).

Many years later, in her home in Via Principessa Clotilde, Maria Montessori would receive Queen Margherita frequently. She also helped Montessori financially and attended the first day of the International Training Course held in Rome.

There were ninety people from different parts of the world who attended the first international course held in January 1913. The majority of them came from America, and the others from Germany, Switzerland, Norway, Sweden, Spain, Portugal, India, China, Japan, Brazil, Chile, Argentina, Canada, and Mexico. They had read her book, now translated in several languages, and came to learn more. Anna Macherroni writes:

Maria Montessori reading a new edition of her book (1913)

"The lecture-room had a singular shape. At one corner was an alcove in which was Dr. Montessori's platform. About a hundred people could sit comfortably" (p. 39).

Montessori had lost her mother in December 1912 and was still in mourning when the course began. "She had ready little cards with her mother's photograph (santino) and gave one to each student" (Maccheroni, p. 39). It was not long after that her son, Mario Montessori came to live with her.[1]

Montessori expressed to her friend Marchesa Maria Maraini Guerrieri-Gonzaga her anxiety before the course began:

Maria Montessori in Piazza del Popolo, Rome (1930) (Maria Montessori Archives, Amsterdam)

In the same spot as Montessori!

"...I am about to appear before an international tribunal to explain that work which benefits others and is fed by my blood!" (2013, p. xvii).

It was her friend who opened the course with a splendid reception in her home. Montessori was well prepared for the course having engaged the services of a Roman company of stenographers, including Antonio Corradini, to transcribe the lectures and type them out. They were later put together as a book and that still exists today. There were also two students who translated the Italian lectures into English for the benefit of the international body of students present at the course.

The first international course began with an introduction by the Roman archaeologist Giacomo Boni (1859-1925). He spoke to the students about Roman art and

---

[1] In 1898, Maria gave birth to Mario, following her relationship with Giusseppe Montesano. She gave up her child for adoption only to be reunited with him in 1913.

took them for a walk to the Roman Forum and the Palantine Hill. Montessori was keen to give her international students a taste of Italian art which no doubt surrounded them too in the nearby Piazza del Popolo with its twin churches Santa Maria dei Miracoli and Santa Maria in Montesanto. Another hidden gem that I visited is the plainer looking basilica, Santa Maria del Popolo, that is designed by Bernini and has some masterpieces by Annibale Carracci and Caravaggio.

Introducing her new experimental science, Maria Montessori says:

> "I repeat and insist: I did not wish to originate a method of education, nor am I the author of a method of education. I have helped some children to live, and I have set forth the means, which I found necessary, and these means are a method of education. And if these means of help are a method of education for children of this age, then all aids to the development of humanity are also methods of education" (2013, p. 10).

Montessori was always observing and learning from the children, and once in these Pincian gardens she witnessed something that left a major impact on her and is an inherent part of her philosophy. She writes:

> "...I saw a baby of about a year and a half, a beautiful smiling child, who was working away trying to fill a little pail by shoveling gravel into it... It was time to go home and the nurse was patiently exhorting the baby to leave his work and let her put him into the baby-carriage. Seeing that her exhortations made no impression on the little fellow's firmness, she herself filled the pail with gravel and set pail and baby into the carriage with the fixed conviction that she had given him what he wanted" (1912, p. 355).

The child reacted by crying loudly and Montessori understood that his purpose was not to fill the pail of gravel but to go through the motions of filling it "thus satisfying a need of his vigorous organism. The child's unconscious aim was his own self-development; not the external fact of a pail full of little stones" (1912, p. 355). Inherent to the Montessori philosophy is the understanding that it is the process, not the product, that is important to the child as they develop and hone their skills.

Montessori was also designing new materials, more advanced apparatus at this time. "There were plane insets, bead bars, chains, squares and cubes for teaching multiplication, fractions, geometry, but, once again, Montessori had difficulty finding workmen willing to take the time and trouble to produce the equipment she had designed" (Kramer, 1976, p. 149). Anna Maccheroni writes:

> "I remember when she showed to a young ironmonger the plane insets for geometry and fractions. The workman refused to do such a work. 'You can cut them out of cardboard,' he said. But when she explained to him the use of them; it was almost a lesson on geometry. The young man liked it and decided to do the work. As for the bead-bars, chains, squares, cubes, the workmen had a great deal to discuss before they were induced to make them" (p. 40).

Montessori ran two classes in her apartment—one for poor children and the other for children of rich families with whom she was experimenting with her more advanced mathematics materials. She also began to work with older children.

In 1910, an American journalist by the name of S.S. McClure, founder and publisher of *McClure's Magazine*, met with Maria Montessori in her home and they embarked on a five-year collaboration to introduce Montessori's innovative style

View of Maria Montessori's home from Piazza del Popolo, Rome

in the United States. It was in 1913, after the success of her first international training course, when McClure came to visit Montessori again that she gave him her power of attorney and decided to travel to the United States.

Acknowledgements:
Martina Crescenzi, Arianna Romoli, Paola Trabalzini and Elena Dompe, Opera Nazionale Montessori Rome

Chapter 7
The "Educational Wonder Worker" Comes to America

S.S. McClure and Maria Montessori during her American
lecture tour, December 1913. McClure captioned this picture:
"For the conquest of the world" (Maria Montessori Archives
Amsterdam)

In the United States, news of Montessori education had spread far and wide by 1911. In an article published in the very popular *McClure's Magazine*, Maria Montessori was described as "an educational wonder worker" and depicted the students studying in her school as "miracle children" because of their ability to read and write at such a young age. "The most conspicuous of Maria Montessori's triumphs is that of teaching quite young children, without putting the smallest strain upon their faculties, first to write and then to read – for her method inverts the usual order in which these accomplishments are acquired" (Tozier, May 1911). She included a photograph of a young child writing on the blackboard with the following caption under it: "ONE OF MARIA MONTESSORI'S PUPILS WRITING FROM DICTATION AT THE BLACKBOARD. THE AVERAGE CHILD OF FOUR LEARNS TO WRITE IN SIX WEEKS BY THE MONTESSORI METHOD. This caption seems to be what fascinated so many of the readers" (Povell, 2010, p. 94). Tozier goes on to discuss Montessori's sensorial activities, how children correct their own mistakes, the educative value of silence, auto education, and quotes Montessori saying, "An axiom of our practical pedagogy is to aid the child only to be independent. He does not wish help" (May 1911).

The American response to the article was intense and positive. "McClure's office was deluged with letters of inquiry as was Montessori herself, in Rome. McClure concluded, 'It seemed as if people everywhere had been waiting for her message'" (Povell, 2010, p. 95). S.S. McClure, the owner and publisher of the magazine, assumed the role of American promoter of the methodology and began running letters from the public commenting on Montessori's ideas in a column that became a regular feature of his magazine. In October 1911, McClure informed his readers that Dr. Montessori's book was soon to be published and promised to run a series of articles describing the method in great detail. The excitement and anticipation was mounting.

An American Montessori school opened in Scarborough, New York, in the fall of 1911, less than six months after the first article appeared in McClure's Magazine. This was in the home of Frank Vanderlip, one of the leading bankers in the country. The teacher in this school was Anne George who was Dr. Montessori's first American pupil and the first teacher to apply the Montessori method in the United States. She had heard from a friend about an opportunity to learn in Italy from Maria Montessori about the self-development and self-mastery of children in primary education She was so impressed with this that she went to Italy to learn about the method first hand. Of her own school she reported:

> "This school, unlike Montessori's first school in Rome, drew its students from cultured families, whose greatest ambition it was to give their children everything possible in the way of education and rational enjoyment" (Povell, 2010, p. 95).

In other words, the American version of Montessori differed from its Italian forerunner as it was not born out of a social initiative even though it was the "miracle children" who had captured the attention of the wealthy Americans. Rita Kramer writes,

The first Montessori School in America run by Anne George

"It was a newsworthy experiment, and accounts of her success in transplanting the Italian educator's methods to a new culture, among upper middle-class children in a beautiful house overlooking the Hudson, appeared in profusely illustrated detail in The New York Times in the winter of 1911 and in an article by Anne George entitled "The First Montessori School in America" in McClure's in June 1912, as well as in a piece published the following month in Good Housekeeping" (1976, p. 163-164).

Soon after, there were additional Montessori schools that opened around the country. Mabel Bell and her spouse, Alexander Graham Bell, inventor of the telephone, were strong supporters and opened Montessori schools in Nova Scotia (summer of 1912) and Washington D.C. (fall of 1912). By December 1911, *McClure Magazine* reported that Montessori schools had opened in Boston and New York "and in response to the clamor for instruction, Montessori would give a course for teachers that winter. It also noted the manufacturer (House of Childhood) hoped to have the didactic apparatus ready for parents and teachers by the beginning of the year (1912)" (Povell, 2010, p. 96).

In the years 1912-1914, there were over 150 English articles and books on Montessori education published in the United States. The first edition of *The Montessori Method* appeared in April 1912, and 5000 copies were sold in four days. Other books about Montessori's work began to appear, and one of the first was Dorothy Canfield Fisher's *A Montessori Mother* (1912). Fisher had visited Rome, met with Montessori and visited the Montessori school at the Franciscan Convent on the Via Giusti. When she returned to the United States, she wrote her book in which she said:

> "Over there in Rome, in a tenement house, a woman doctor begins observations in an experimental laboratory of children, and in five years' time, which is nothing to a real scientist, her laboratory doors are stormed by

inquirers from Australia, from Norway, from Mexico, and, most of all from the United States. Teachers of district schools in the Carolinas write their cousins touring Europe to be sure to go to Rome to see the Montessori schools. Mothers from Oregon and Maine write, addressing their letters, 'Montessori, Rome'" (Fisher, 1912, p. 224).

Fisher's efforts to put Montessori education into an American context did not go well with Montessori. She wrote, "I have not deputed – and do not propose to depute – to others the work of a practical popular explanation of my method, as I have taken great pains to do this myself. I hope my system will not be held responsible for any want of success that may arise out of the use of other books" (Povell, 2010, p. 98). The success of her method had the world curious and this led Montessori to insist that only she would speak about her Method of education. She was not supportive of others who tried to do so on her behalf.

Montessori received many invitations to come to the United States to visit the American schools and to lecture, but she consistently refused. In December 1912, her mother died and Montessori found solace in work. She held the first International Training Course in Rome in 1913 with more than one hundred pupils from various countries. The greatest representation was from the United States with sixty-seven students. Some of the students who took this course became close associates of Montessori and life long friends – Helen Parkhurst, Adelia McAlpin Pyle and Claude Claremont.

In the fall of 1913, facing financial difficulties arising from bad investments, S.S. McClure was forced to sell his magazine and do a lecture tour around the country. This is when he came up with the idea that he would travel to Rome and try to convince Dr. Montessori to come to America. McClure's biographer wrote,

"McClure traveled to Rome in the fall of 1913 to broach and subsequently clinch the deal. In the view of the Dottoressa, grateful for the attention given her work in *McClure's Magazine*, S.S. was a rich and powerful protector who could do no wrong" (Povell, 2010, p. 98). Montessori had prepared some films showing her children at work and McClure planned a lecture series in the USA which would feature her method and the film she had produced. Montessori was attracted to McClure's vision and agreed to his plan. McClure wrote to his wife from Rome on November 15, 1913, "I think it will be a money maker".

E.M. Standing writes about a prophetic dream Montessori had:

> "One night – it was during her second international course held at Rome in 1914 – Dr. Montessori had an unusually vivid dream. She dreamt that she was in a rowing boat on the Atlantic, and that she was making her way in it to America. In her dream she remarked to herself, "I had no idea it was so easy to get to America!" (1957, p. 62).

In the diary that Dr. Montessori kept during her first voyage to America in 1913, she is excited about her upcoming visit and at the same time sad to leave her son, Mario (aged 15 years), behind. Mario had left his boarding school in February 1913 and joined his mother at Via Principessa Clotilde in Rome. As she leaves him with her father, she writes:

> "I saw my heroic child waving goodbye and comforting me from the quay. He jumped up and down, puffed out his cheeks and shouted: I am happy! His voice reached me even when I could no longer see him" (2013, p. 1).

She speaks highly of McClure:

> "McClure is completely captivated by the project: he is thinking and studying all the time. He speaks to everybody about it. Everyday he comes up with new ideas – full of enthusiasm and confidence. He calls the decision to make this trip a miracle and a godsend, of which the splendid and fortunate consequences cannot be predicted" (2013, p. 30).

On December 4th, 1913, *The New York Herald* announced her arrival: "Dr. Montessori, Italian Educator comes to promote her ideals". Exciting times lay ahead for Montessori and among them was a meeting with President Wilson.

As they disembarked from the Cincinnati, "all eyes were on them – Montessori, the great educator, and McClure, the famous editor and publisher" (Gutek, 2016, p. 122). There were press conferences that followed, and since Dr. Montessori did not speak English, her first American student, Anne George, became her translator. The reviews that followed were very complimentary. The Times published an article in bold letters, enticing the readers: "DR. MONTESSORI TALKS OF HER MODE OF 'AUTOEDUCATION'", and goes on to describe her personality as such:

> "But she gives, above all, the impression of poise and sureness. It is perhaps that contrasted with our own nervousness, perhaps the mere fact that she is in a strange country and does not understand English – whatever the cause, she seems curiously detached. She is not aloof, she is interested in this odd and noisy place, but she is always apart, serene and untouched by it" (New York Times, December 7th, 1913).

She had a very demanding schedule. "Returning from her gala reception in Washington, Montessori's next schedule event was a

Carnegie Hall, New York

lecture at Carnegie Hall in New York City on December 8" (Gutek, 2016, p. 135). It was a sold-out evening with The New York Times reporting that over one thousand people had been turned away. There was a large banner overhead that read, "America Welcomes Dottoressa Montessori". John Dewey, American philosopher of education and professor at Columbia University, presided over the event and welcomed Montessori.

Dr. Montessori, dressed in black, still in mourning over the death of her mother, came to the stage amidst all the applause. She spoke in Italian about how she developed her method at the Casa dei Bambini in Rome. "She emphasized the importance of applying science to education and how her insights had come from the empirical observation of children at work and at play... Montessori emphasized that children needed the freedom to act on their innermost impulses to work; through work, they developed themselves" (Gutek, 2016, p. 135). It was at the end of this two-hour address that Montessori concluded, "My larger aim is the eventual perfection of the human race" (2016, p. 136). On the heels of the resounding success at Carnegie Hall, McClure and his manager, Lee Keedick, organized another lecture there on December 15th. In the meanwhile, Montessori went on to Philadelphia. It was a tightly scheduled and stressful tour but everyone involved was pleased at how successful it was. "Montessori reported that she found the schools in America faithful to her method. After a successful lecture tour she left the United States at the end of December, 1913" (Povell, 2010, p. 90).

After her departure, McClure continued lecturing and showing the films for which he had acquired rights from Dr. Montessori. McClure's biographer, Peter Lyon, described what happened, "behind the scenes there had been an unseemly scramble to exploit the Dottoressa, her Method, her apparatus, and everything else involved. McClure had scrambled with the others" (Povell, 2010, p. 99-100). The actual cause of the Montessori-McClure

The Flat Iron Building in New York where the House of Childhood was located

break up was financial – he was taking a 20% of the net proceeds, another 20% went to his manager, Lee Keedick, and Montessori got the remaining 60%. "The House of Childhood, the company that manufactured and sold Montessori's didactic apparatus in the United States, was a pivotal financial issue with unfortunate consequences for the business relationship between Montessori and McClure" (Gutek, 2016, p. 151).

Montessori believed that she was being taken advantage of. More problems arose when she felt she did not get her share of the money raised from the American lecture tour. She felt cheated. All her travel expenses and those of her companions were deducted from her share of the profits. She was expecting 60% of the profits after the expenses were deducted. After this, Montessori became very suspicious of McClure and forbid him from publishing the lectures from the tour. She sent a telegram to McClure in April 1914: "DO NOT DO ANYTHING WITHOUT REGULAR CONTRACTS FORBID PUBLICATION LAST YEARS LECTURES" (Gutek, 2016, p. 169). It was clear that Montessori did not trust McClure anymore. She had a problem with him using her films and repeatedly requesting the negatives. McClure sent his brother, Robert, to Rome for further negotiations, but Montessori did not like that. Robert wrote to his brother, "I cannot help thinking someone in America has been poisoning her mind and that influence together with this distrustful attitude of her entourage in Rome has made her thoroughly dissatisfied with her arrangement with you" (Povell, 2010, p. 100). Lengthy talks followed but came to an impasse. Montessori demanded dissolving the Montessori Society of America and canceling all contracts, lectures, and films. The relationship had deteriorated too far to be functional any more. McClure sailed to his hometown in Ireland, and his wife, Harriet, closed up the business relationship with Maria Montessori in the spring of 1914.

In the aftermath, Montessori education that had reached its

Maria Montessori gives a lecture in Italian to 5,000 teachers in Los Angeles, California, in 1915. The English translator is Adelia Pyle (Maria Montessori Archives Amsterdam)

peak in the United States in 1913 began to decline. John Dewey and his pragmatic approach gained more support in the light of William Kilpatrick's critique of The Montessori Method. In *The Montessori System Examined* in 1914, he "dismissed Montessori's assertion that her method was based on scientific findings. Kilpatrick found her method was deeply flawed by her limited knowledge of contemporary educational psychology... It was, he wrote in a mid-nineteenth century piece 'fifty years behind' modern educational thought" (Gutek, 2016, p. 188).

Montessori did come to America again but it was not on an invitation by McClure or the Montessori Educational Association. She came to California to lecture and to set up a demonstration school at the Panama-Pacific International Exposition. War was raging in Europe and the identity of her sponsors was not clear. It has been suggested that The National Education Association and one of her pupils, Catherine Moore from Los Angeles, convinced her to come. Montessori's funding was much less than it had been during the 1913 tour and even though articles did appear about her in the newspapers, it was significantly less than the first time around.

Montessori arrived in New York City on April 18th, 1915 along with her son Mario, now seventeen years old, and Anna Fedeli. Adelia McAlpin Pyle and Helen Parkhurst, who Montessori

Glass-walled demonstration classroom in the Palace of Education at the Panama Pacific International Exposition, San Francisco 1915 (Maria Montessori Archives, Amsterdam, the Netherlands)

had trained in Rome in 1914, joined them in Chicago. Anne George, who played a significant role in the 1913 Lecture Tour, was not involved this time around. Montessori first went to Los Angeles and delivered the third international training course (May 1-July 28, 1915).

She then went to San Francisco where she conducted her fourth international training course from August 1 – November 30. She began her lecture series with:

> "The characteristic fact in this method of education is that instead of having the teacher who instructs the children or guides them step by step, we substitute materials for development and we emphasize organization of work studied in a positive and experimental way so that it corresponds to the spontaneous activities of the child" (2008, p. 60).

This time around her students were able to see firsthand what Montessori was describing.

"One of the noteworthy aspects of Montessori's second visit was the glass-walled model demonstration school that she set up in the expositions' Palace of Education and Social Economy" (Gutek, 2016, p. 191). The glass classroom had many visitors between August and November who came to see the twenty-one children between the ages of three and six work in a Montessori classroom. These children had been selected out of a pool of two thousand applicants. Helen Parkhurst worked as the Directress under Montessori's supervision.

In a letter to her father, Montessori writes,

> "Inside the Palace of Education, on a raised platform about one metre from the ground, there is a Casa dei Bambini. (The Italian name has been written in large letters outside the class and will remain Italian, just as the German word Kindergarten is always used for the Froebel classes.) Its walls are made of glass: the Glass Class is much admired here at the Exposition. The inside is grey-blue and decorated with all kinds of fresh pin flowers; even the teacher is dressed in pink. Inside there are thirty children, chosen from the 2,500 that asked for admission, working enchantingly, while outside large groups of people crowd together and stay there for hours on end to watch. Even when school is over, the people stay there, gazing

Glass Classroom (1915)

at the emptiness, almost as if they are seeing something extraordinary. The next day they are back, long before the children arrive" (2015, p. 69).

In 1913, Montessori had relied on the motion pictures of her school in Rome, but now she had a classroom that showcased all that she lectured about—children working with the didactic apparatus. Her new book *Dr. Montessori's Own Handbook*, was published and she made it very clear that hers was the only authentic voice of the Method. An introduction to the book reads:

"As a result of the widespread interest that has been taken in my method of child education, certain books have been issued, which may appear to the general reader to be authoritative expositions of the Montessori system. I wish to state definitely that the present work, the English translation of which has been authorized and approved by me, is the only authentic manual of the Montessori method, and that the only other authentic or authorized works of mine in the English language are 'The Montessori Method', and 'Pedagogical Anthropology'" (Gutek, 2016, p. 191-192).

Maria Montessori returned to Europe on December 8th, 1915. By 1916-1917, there were over 100 Montessori school in 22 states. However, the movement died down just as quickly as it had started. There were multiple reasons that led to its decline, and of course the main one was the First World War that caused travel limitations and an anti-immigrant sentiment. By the 1920s, Montessori schools had all but disappeared from the United States and did not return until the 1950s.

On her return from the USA, Dr. Montessori based herself in Barcelona, Spain where a Seminari-Laboratori de Pedagogia had been created for her.

Panama Pacific International Exhibition Grounds then (1915) and now (2018)

Chapter 8
"She was ours":
Maria Montessori's
Barcelona Years

Montessori school in Barcelona 1932-1934

By the start of the 1920s, Dr. Maria Montessori had built quite a reputation around the world. The first *Casa dei Bambini* (Children's House) opened in 1907 in a working–class neighborhood in Rome, and within a short period of time there were schools following her method, not only in Europe, but also in the United States, Asia, and Central and South America. Simultaneously, Montessori was also offering courses for teachers and writing articles in Italian and English to publicize her method and thought. Fame and recognition came quickly to Montessori. The world's press recorded stories of how successful her methods were, and cultural leaders bestowed favors on her, and supported the growth of her educational system.

However, when the Fascist rule became dominant in Italy, Maria Montessori saw that her ideas of education could not work in this authoritarian atmosphere. She realized that schools were part of the social mechanism that conditioned people toward an acceptance of war, prejudice, hatred, and violence. This was in conflict with the social ethos of her schools that reflected a concern for civic virtue and incorporated this by teaching peace, respect, grace, and courtesy—the skills needed to resolve conflicts in an orderly and dignified manner.

> "Indeed, the Fascists ordered all her schools to be closed down. In Germany and Austria – then under Nazi rule – things were even more drastic. An effigy of Montessori was burned over a pyre of her own books in a public square both in Berlin and Vienna" (Standing, p. 85).

So, when Montessori returned to Europe at the end of her second American trip, she took the invitation of local government officials in Barcelona and made Spain her home.

The Spanish magazine *Feminal* had published an article on the Montessori method on September 24th, 1911. It "presented the method's characteristics and highlighted the fact that by

Casa de Maternidad, Barcelona

giving children freedom, Montessori managed to maintain a high degree of discipline among them" (Rubi & Garcia, 2011). The first Montessori school in Spain was started in Barcelona in 1913 when Spain came to realize that the answer to its need for modernization lay in improving its educational system. In 1913, the Barcelona Provincial Council began to reform the *Casa de Maternidad* from a gloomy orphanage to an institution where the most economically disadvantaged children could receive care based on the principles inspired by Montessori's ideas. "Although the project could not be developed in its entirety, the nursery at the *Casa de Materinidad* would become a frame for disseminating Montessori's pedagogical ideas from 1914 onward" (Rubi & Garcia, 2011).

Casa dels nens, Barcelona

John Palau Vera, a teacher who attended the first International Montessori Course in Rome in 1913, played a large role in publicizing the Montessori method in Barcelona. While the pilot project at the *Casa de Materinidad* was being launched, the Barcelona Provincial Council provided grants for seven teachers to attend the second International Montessori Course in Rome. Palau Vera also received Montessori's permission to translate her writings into Spanish, and this helped to popularize her work even more.

In 1915, just as Maria Montessori left for America, she sent Anna Maccheroni, who had worked with her from the start, to Barcelona, where a small school with just five children opened. This was the *Casa dels nens* (Carrer Universitat # 21).

The school became popular very quickly and within six months already had over one hundred children.

"There had been no attempt to publicize the school and no promotion was undertaken; there were no prospectuses and no newspaper articles. The parents of the original five children told others, who brought their children to the school and asked that they be allowed to attend" (Kramer, 1976, p. 248).

Larger premises were needed to accommodate the growing numbers and the school moved to Carrer de la Diputacio #262.

Carrer de la Diputacio, Barcelona

Carrer d'Aribau 155, Barcelona

Around this time, Anna Maccheroni was invited by the Abbot of the Benedictine Order to take part in a Liturgical Congress in Montserrat. Maccheroni felt that the teaching of the Liturgy could be presented to the children and announced that she was ready to try out the experiment in the model Montessori school in Barcelona. With this, religious education in Montessori schools began, and in 1930, "The Child in the Church" was published. Montessori schools were gaining in popularity and the City Montessori School opened at Carrer d'Aribau 155.

Plans were made for Maria Montessori to give a training course in Barcelona in mid-February 1916, and so when Montessori returned from California she moved to Barcelona to prepare for this.

There were 185 attendees from Europe, Australia, and North America who came to learn the theoretical and practical components of the Montessori method. As a result of this course, the Association of Friends of the Montessori Method was created. The Catalan government, very interested in educational reform, fully backed and supported Maria Montessori.

Newspaper clipping announcing the 18th International Teacher Training Course in Barcelona

82

Her popularity grew, with people expressing their admiration for her and inviting her to visit their schools. So much so that once when she could not hold back her tears in church and later apologized for breaking down, she was told not to be sorry for "She had cried with us, she was ours" (Kramer, 1976). Such was her acceptance!

For Montessori,

> "...it seemed, she had finally found the opportunity she had been waiting for, the chance to experiment on a large scale under her own control with the application of her method to children of various ages and backgrounds, and to extend the method into the program of the elementary-school years" (Kramer, 1976, p. 248).

The Seminari Laboratori de Pedagogia (Diagonal 482) training and research center, as well as a school, was the perfect setting which the Catalan government gave to Maria Montessori to continue with her work.

"The institute was housed in an old building of traditional Spanish architecture with spacious grounds, gardens, orchards, and winding, palm-lined paths. There were little pools with fountains and goldfish, sheds and cages for pets, all under the brilliant southern sky" (Kramer, 1976, p. 250).

Around 1920, the Catalan independence movement

Seminari Laboratori de Pedagogia, Barcelona

ESCAPE FROM SPAIN

ITALIAN WOMAN TELLS THRILLING STORY

Drive to Cruiser with British Flag Flying

Dr Maria Montessori, the eminent Italian specialist in child psychology and education, told to-day a thrilling story of how she got away from Spain.

She was lecturing at the City of London vacation course in Education. Dr Montessori, who had been living in Spain lately, said that churches in Barcelona were on fire when she left.

"I do not think I was ever in danger," she said. "Barcelona was still in Government hands, but the priests had taken an active part in the fighting, and I believe most of the danger to the churches was caused by stocks of ammunition left inside by them.

Armed Escort.

"When an armed escort arrived at my house I thought I was to be taken to a prison, but they assured me that I was safe. 'We are not killing women,' they said.

"Just then the British Consul's car arrived and I was told to make immediate preparations for my journey to London.

"I packed, and within a few minutes we were driving down to the quay-side with the British flag flying prominently on the front of the car."

"The British cruiser Douglas was waiting there, and I was taken on board, received by the commander, and then taken to a cabin. I was the only foreigner and the only woman on board. We left immediately for Marseilles."

Holiday for Children.

Dr Montessori is grey-haired and is over 60 years of age. She lectures in Italian with great vigour, and to-day she described her plan for "education of independence" in children.

She advocated, among other things, a two years' holiday for all normal children from the age of twelve.

She is a president of the International Montessori Association, which holds its fifth congress in Oxford next week.

She is a Doctor of Medicine of Rome University and an Honorary Doctor of Literature of Durham.

began to demand that Montessori take a political stand and make a public statement favoring Catalan independence, but Montessori refused to do so. Official support was withdrawn from her programs. In 1924, a new military dictatorship closed Montessori's model school in Barcelona, and Montessori education declined in Spain, although Barcelona remained Montessori's home for the next twelve years. In 1933, under the Second Spanish Republic, the government sponsored a new training course and government support was re-established. However, with the onset of the Spanish Civil War in 1936, the political and social conditions drove Montessori to leave Spain permanently. She left Barcelona aboard a British warship for England where she and Mario took refuge. As Montessori herself stated in an English newspaper:

"I do not think I was ever in danger. Barcelona was still in Government hands, but the priests had taken an active part in the fighting, and I believe most of the danger to the churches was caused by stocks of ammunition left inside by them. When an armed escort arrived at my house I thought I was to be taken to a prison, but they assured me that I was safe. 'We are not killing women,' they said.

Just then the British Consul's car arrived and I was told to make immediate preparations for my journey to London. I packed, and within a few minutes we were driving down to the quay-side with the British flag flying prominently on the front of the car.

The British cruiser Douglas was waiting there and I was taken on board, received by the commander, and then taken to a cabin. I was the only foreigner and the only woman on board. We left immediately for Marseilles" (London Evening Telegraph, August 3, 1936).

From England Maria and Mario Montessori traveled to the Netherlands to stay with the family of Ada Pierson. Ada Pierson was the daughter of a Dutch banker and later became the second wife of Mario Montessori.

Acknowledgements:
Fina Solà i Gasset, Diputació de Barcelona
Joke Verheul, Association Montessori Internationale, The Netherlands

Montessori school in Barcelona 1932-1934

Chapter 9
"We'll talk later..."
Maria Montessori in Laren

Groenendaal School, Laren

W ith the onset of the Spanish Civil War in 1936, the political and social conditions in Spain drove Maria Montessori to leave what had become her home since 1916. She left Barcelona aboard a British warship and arrived in England with "no definite plans for their immediate future, no clear idea of where to settle next" (Kramer, 1976, p. 337). Among the many friends and associates of the Montessori family who insisted they come and stay with them was Ada Pierson.

Ada Pierson, daughter of a Dutch banker, had taken the Montessori training course in England and now urged Montessori to come to Holland. Her family home was in Baarn, outside Amsterdam, and on the invitation of the Pierson family, Maria Montessori, Mario, and Mario's children came to live in the Intimis villa for a few months. It was here that Dr. Montessori completed her book *The Secret of Childhood*, and dedicated it to her hosts, the Pierson family. By the end of 1936, they moved to Laren, and with the help of friends and supporters opened a Montessori school. *De Binckhorst* became her home from 1936-1939 and initially she lived upstairs and housed a little casa downstairs.

The Casa at De Binckjhorst, Laren

Within a short period of time, the Casa was full and more space was needed. A short walk away from *De Binckhorst* a much bigger school was founded with a casa, an elementary school, a teacher training college, and a department for special education. "The plan was for Montessori to teach there during five months of each year, reserving her other time for training courses elsewhere, continuing to travel and lecture, organize congresses and oversee the worldwide Montessori society activities" (Kramer, 1976, p. 338). For Dr. Montessori, it was the happiest time in her life. It seemed as though the work she had started in Barcelona could be continued, away from the social upheavals that Europe was facing.

"Laren was like a benign little island apart from the bitter struggles of the outside world" (Kramer, 1976, p. 339). Serene and idyllic in its setting, it transported me to another world, very different from Amsterdam, and reminded me of my childhood. Margot Waltuch writing in *A Montessori Album: Reminiscences of a Montessori Life*, describes the location as, "The outdoor space surrounding our school and research center in Laren in the Netherlands had nothing spectacular to show – just grass, a few beautiful trees, a small pond and two colorful ducks" (1986, p. 24). The lake takes one's breath away and just opposite what was the school is now a deer park!

Laren

It was here in *Groenendaal* that many of the Montessori materials, including Geography and Botany, were developed. I remember Margot Waltuch relating the tale of how the Leaf Cabinet came to be. She spoke about a fall morning when the children were having lots of fun with the leaves: piling them into big heaps and, as children do, jumping into them, over them, throwing them in the air and trying to catch them. It was during a morning like this that Dr. Montessori came by, stood and watched the children in this activity. Margot Waltuch writes, "She stood next to us-pensive, serious. Her facial expression could not hide anything, and I, a very young, inexperienced teacher, began to wonder. What did I do wrong? I asked her. She shook her head and said, "We'll talk later" (1986, p. 24). I have often wondered how I would have reacted to that comment!

"Later," Dr. Montessori explained so clearly: "Everything is fine, the children enjoyed the experience, but this is only one side of the picture. The colors of the leaves, their weight, their rustling, their textures, and their smell are the sensorial level only. What did you teach them?" (Waltuch, 1986, p. 24). This got Margot Waltuch thinking, as I am sure it would any other teacher in this situation. How could this sensorial experience be more fruitful to the child? She began by drawing the parts of a leaf and presented it the following morning to children between 7-8 years old. They showed little interest in the activity, and on Montessori's suggestion she then presented it to younger children (5-7 year olds). However, it was when she presented it to the 3-4.5 year olds that the activity gained "real interest, repetition and joy of learning" (1986, p. 24). Sure enough, a hundred years later, the children at Montessori Casa International find the terminology cards of the leaf (and others) just as interesting. They match the three part cards, learn the names of the different parts, meticulously count the number of pages needed to make their own booklet, fetch them along with the right colored pencils, and create their own little nomenclature books. Over the three years that they are in Primary, their coloring improves, and so does their handwriting, but they never tire of creating the same book over and over again, each time perfecting the art.

Terminology cards of a leaf

According to Margot Waltuch, this was the beginning of the Montessori botany work. The classified nomenclature cards led to the creation of the leaf cabinet, "a wooden cabinet of three drawers containing 14 leaf-shaped insets with wooden frames. The study of leaves launched

Leaf Cabinet

the children into a detailed and particular exploration of the plant world" (1986, p. 24).

Unfortunately, *Groenendaal*, where the beginnings of Montessori geography and botany work took place, was shut down during the Second World War. The Germans closed the school, and after the war *Groenendaal* was torn down. The only thing that is left is a shield on the gate.

The war convinced Montessori that the only way to bring peace in the world was to educate the children. With this in mind, she designed a curriculum that emphasized the interdependence of everyone and everything. The "prepared paths to culture" that lead children from sensory exploration to educational knowledge (as shown in the experiment with the leaves) and "cosmic education" as we now know it began in Laren, Holland.

At Groendaal, Laren

"All is strictly interrelated on this planet... each detail holds the child's interest by reason of its strict relation to the others. We may compare it with a tapestry: each detail is a piece of embroidery; the whole constitutes a magnificent cloth" (Montessori 1948/1973, p. 39).

In 1939, with the threat of war imminent, Maria and Mario Montessori left Europe for India on an invitation to teach a 3-month training course in Chennai.

Acknowledgements:
Joke Verheul, Association Montessori Internationale, The Netherlands

Chapter 10
The Light of India:
A Twinkle in the Eye

Children working in the Olcott Bungalow with Maria Montessori as the observor

I have been told I need to meet Raji teacher.

Before I know it, an older woman ushers me into a small red car and we careen down the back alleys of Chennai, India. We arrive at a garden-level flat where two grinning women in earthy silk saris and jasmine flowers dangling from their hair greet us. Immediately, these three women are gossiping and giggling like schoolgirls in the playground as they recall their encounters with a woman they call "Madam".

For the rest of us, we know "Madam" with the slightly more formal title of Dr. Maria Montessori.

I am here in the south of India during the final stage of my Montessori pilgrimage. I have been involved in Montessori education since 1984 and have since traveled to many significant Montessori sites in Italy and the Netherlands. As a lifelong learner of the Montessori philosophy, I am looking for a deeper understanding of how and why Montessori developed the spiritual dimension to her method and her vision of cosmic education. I have read that the inspiration for both had come from this lush region that tumbles down into the Indian Ocean.

Olcott Bungalow, Chennai

At the age of 69, "Maria Montessori began one of the most interesting and important phases of her already remarkable life" (Standing, 1957, p. 70) when the Theosophical Society of India extended an invitation to the Montessoris to journey to India and to give lectures and training courses. World War II had just broken out and Montessori was forced into exile from Italy because of her liberal and antifascist views. Montessori accepted the invitation and reached India in 1939.

Theosohical Society, Chennai

I was watching the three women's animated faces without really listening, when suddenly my ears perked up. They were reminiscing about the time they were asked to assemble a guard of honor for Montessori and her son, Mario. Their voices swelled with pride as they recounted how children stood waving on both sides of the road from the gates of the Theosophical Society to the Olcott Bungalow.

Earlier in the day I had met Mr. C. Nachiappan, founder of Kalakshetra Publications (the first publishers of Montessori texts) and a strong supporter of the Montessori movement, who told me that Dr. Montessori had been received with "such an august welcome only given to very few people in those days". He had been at the airport and witnessed the arrival of the Montessoris in Chennai: "She arrived in Madras via Bombay in November 1939. She came on a mail plane that was personally piloted by JRD Tata." Every Indian knows JRD Tata; he was one of the most enterprising Indian entrepreneurs and built the largest industrial house of India! The fact that he personally flew the Montessoris to Madras (now Chennai) makes it quite obvious that her arrival in India was a matter of huge significance and that she was greeted as a very special guest. Nachiappan continued to describe the event, "Children were lined up along both sides of the road and waving out to her".

The Theosophical Society is nestled within 250 acres of vibrant green trees and plants, including a 500-year-old banyan tree, under which Montessori is known to have held discourses with many notable personalities. As we walked along the grounds toward the banyan tree, I was amazed at the diversity of nature and the serenity and solitude it provided. Away from the noise of the city and people, this was a sanctuary and I found myself at once at peace in this tranquility. I thought of Montessori and what this place must have done for her away from the wars that the Western world was fighting.

Banyan Tree, Theosophical Society Chennai

I was given a brief introduction to the aims of the Theosophical Society and immediately I could see similarities with the Montessori Philosophy: respect for all things, freedom of thought, and development of latent potentialities in individuals. The banyan tree was amazing. The parent tree is now dead but the rest of the tree sprawls around a huge area. In honor of my teacher, I hung a "mallai" on the tree. In South India, the flower garland, or "mallai", is presented to gods and people of honor. In quite a few pictures of Maria Montessori at this time, she is wearing the "mallai" along with the "angavastham" (also given as a symbol of honor).

Olcott Bungalow, Chennai

The three women continued to reminisce about "Madam" and Mario. They chatted about what beautiful human beings they both were and how they genuinely cared about their students. One of the ladies excitedly recalled how she had

Maria and Mario Montessori with George Arundale and Rukhmani Devi (Maria Montessori Archives, Amsterdam)

visited Mario Montessori in Amsterdam many years later and how touched she was that he remembered her and made it a point to ask about many of his students in India. It was also clear that school with the Montessoris was a lot of fun as they discussed the timeline "that was more than a furlong long... we started unrolling it from the gate..." and how that taught them how civilization evolved. Happily they remembered "how we went on long walks to collect leaves and then we dried them and studied them". They spoke proudly about their standard math exams in which they chose questions that no one else attempted because Mario had made math so much fun and they found it very easy.

Ocott Bungalow, Chennai

We then drove to the Olcott Bungalow and were shown the grounds in which the first course was held in 1939. I was told that thatched huts were constructed there to house the 350 students who came to attend the course, and the largest of them was used as the lecture hall. Dr. Montessori lectured in Italian, and I asked Bhuvna, who had taken the training under Montessori, if that was a problem. She explained that although Montessori did not lecture in English, she certainly knew the language. She once heard Montessori speak in English and questioned her about her knowledge of the language. To this Montessori replied with a twinkle in her eye, "Only know Italian...very convenient!" Mr. Nachiappan further explained that Mario translated Montessori's lectures into English: the translation was done after every few lines. Dr. Montessori paid very close attention to the translation, and whenever Mario fumbled for words, it was Montessori who provided the suitable English expression! Besides, Bhuvna elaborated, she must have known English for she corrected all their albums. What I would give to hear her speak or watch her give a presentation or two! "Madam had beautiful hands with which she demonstrated her materials," Nachiappan said.

It was hard for me to believe that I was standing in the place that had housed my teacher during World War II; first in the school that had been used as an observatory and practical training school for the Montessoris and the participants in the course, and then in their residential quarters. The Olcott Bungalow is grand with gigantic Roman pillars that once had a great view of the Bay of Bengal. I imagined Maria Montessori in a white "very loose-fitting full-length gown… walking up and down most of the time in the open balcony of the bungalow," Bhuvna said. What had she been thinking as she lived in this foreign country that showered her with respect and strived to meet all of her needs? Did she miss the way of life she was used to? Or was she so absorbed in studying the universal "bambino" that it did not matter to her where she was?

The grounds where the Montessori training course was held in Chennai

Terrace of the Ocott Bungalow, Chennai

The conversation between the three women stirred me toward an answer to these questions: both Montessori and Mario were focused on education and studying the child. "Madam pointed at the child, but the problem today is that most of the people are looking at their fingers and not at what they were pointing at – the child," Bhuvna said. She went on to emphasize how important it is not to lose focus on the child: "Always think of the child," she advised.

Close to the grounds of the Theosophical Society is the Kalakshetra Center, which I also visited. What a place of quiet, beauty, and simplicity. It is truly India at its cultural best, bringing together traditional dance, theatre, music, and art. It reminded me of my visit to Shanktinektan (abode of peace) many years ago. It was here that Rabindranath Tagore[1], started his Patha Bhavana, the schools of his ideals, whose central premise was that learning in a natural environment was more enjoyable and meaningful. I have never forgotten the idyllic existence and experience of watching students taking classes in the outdoors. At Kalakshetra, I was fascinated by the simplicity, dedication, and the relationship between the teacher and the students. I thought of how this place must have influenced Maria Montessori. She speaks of beauty in the classroom as something that is simple and harmonious, not luxurious, and always of respect for the environment and the people in it. Was this the beginning of the spiritual aspect of her teacher training? Could it also be that the idea of the Erdkinder and cosmic education took root here? It may very well have been.

Mario Montessori summed up the significance of their stay in India saying, "And in my heart the light of India steadily warms the sense of gratitude for the country which showed so great a regard for Dr. Montessori, surrounded her with friendship, and gave her the support and collaboration of selflessly devoted students." I feel fortunate that I was able to meet some of the people who supported the Montessoris during their stay in India, share photographs with them, and gain personal insights. As we were leaving, the ladies continued reminiscing, and then Raji teacher was talking of how they had only one chair in their home and out of respect it was reserved for "Madam". In fact, it was called the "Madam Montessori chair".

Dr. Montessori had settled in well in Chennai and was busy giving teacher training courses as well as observing children in the Olcott Bungalow school. A change came when the Theosophical Society was needed as an army base and Maria and

---

[1] Rabindranath Tagore was a poet, musician and artist from India In 1913 he became the first non-European to win the Nobel Prize in Literature. Tagore was the patron of the first Indian Montessori training course in Adyar.

Kalakshetra Center, Chennai

Mario were sent to the hill station of Kodaikanal. With her failing health, the cooler temperatures of Kodaikanal provided a welcome relief to Maria Montessori.

Acknowledgements:
Mrs. V. Bhuvaneswari
Ms. P. K. Rajeswari
Ms. G. Sundari
Mr. C. Nacchaipan
Lt. Col. Nandan and Uma Nilakanta

Chapter 11
Safety and Salvation in Kodaikanal:
The Birth of Cosmic Education

Rose Bank, Kodaikanal

"We had made a new discovery which was special and long-lasting, and it all came about in the hills at Kodaikanal, where practice and ideas met – and a better vision emerged" (Mario Montessori, 1998, p. 42).

Having visited the Olcott Bungalow in Chennai and seen for myself where Maria Montessori had lived during the Second World War, I was now keen to visit Kodaikanal, the birthplace of cosmic education.

When the Theosophical Society became the headquarters of the army, the Montessoris were shifted to a hill station called Kodaikanal. There was growing concern regarding Maria Montessori's health, and the Theosophical Society took the responsibility of moving the Montessoris to "a higher place where there was a better climate" (Montessori, 1998, p. 35.) Mario Montessori wrote about the house (Rose Bank):

Rose Bank, Kodaikanal

"We found a house which met our needs, with a minimum of stairs, a fireplace, a garden in the front, and a garden in back. The garden in the front was on the same level as the house" (1998, p. 35).

Kodaikanal is a tiny mountaintop town known for its rugged beauty with wooded slopes, gorgeous waterfalls, and the beautiful Kodai Lake. It is also renowned for its educational institutions of international repute. About 325 miles from

Chennai, it takes approximately nine hours over winding roads to get to Kodaikanal.

The cooler weather and the scenic beauty must have provided a welcome change to Maria Montessori, but she missed the cultural and political bustle of Chennai. She was no longer training teachers and had no opportunities to work with little children. As she said to her student, Lena Wikramaratne, who followed her to Kodaikanal:

> "What can I do here? I can't give a course; all I can do if you come to me in the evenings is talk and show you some material" (2013, p. 86).

It is during this period and under these circumstances that cosmic education was born. Deprived of the Montessori didactic apparatus to begin with, Mario Montessori and Lena Wikamaratne used nature as their teaching tools. As Ms. Wikramaratne describes:

> "We used to go together and pick the moss and marsh plants and come back and make the terrariums and aquariums. We used to bring samples from nature and keep them to let the children see the different ways of life" (2013, p. 87).

Mario Montessori expounds:

> "So we created these terrariums to show the collaboration between plants and animals. We would catch one animal at a time, observe them in our constructed surroundings and then return them to nature after a while. When the curiosity of the children seemed satisfied, we would move on to a different animal and a different concept" (1998, p. 37).

It was the Kodaikanal experience that generated the theosophical vision of universal unity and the interdependency that exists in nature. It was here that so many of the materials that we use to teach today—botany, the story of the universe, geography charts—were created, and I was keen to see the place where it all began.

However, other than the fact that the Montessoris had resided in a bungalow called "Rose Bank" in Kodaikanal, I had no other information. I did not have the address or any milestone (in India, this is a very common way of telling people where you live!). So whereas we decided to make the drive to Kodaikanal, we were not certain we would find the bungalow. There could have been so many things that might have changed since 1942— among them being that the house might have been renamed or demolished!

Our driver was not very optimistic, but humored me by saying that there was no point worrying about it at the start of our journey. When we got there we would see! As we drove into Kodaikanal, the beauty of the surroundings was truly mesmerizing. I was happy to be away from the heat and pollution of Chennai and could see why this place is often called the "Princess of Hill stations". Our hotel was situated on Kodai Lake, and the beauty of the rolling clouds and serenity of the water took my breath away.

However, my first point of business there was to find "Rose Bank". I headed into the hotel and before checking in, I asked the concierge in a most hesitating way if he knew where "Rose Bank" might be. He shook his head "no", not knowing how upset this was making me, but pointed to the manager's office and suggested I go and ask him. The manager had been there for a longer time than the concierge had, I was told. I promptly made my way to the manager's office and again asked my question, hoping against hope. To my surprise and delight, he nodded, "yes". I could have hugged him, but he was a formal Indian gentleman and, in hindsight, I am so glad I did not! He asked me in a most polite manner if I had a driver, and told me to fetch him so he could give the driver directions. Much head nodding followed as directions were exchanged in the Tamil language, and my driver asked me if I was ready to go. As we got into the car, even my driver was smiling.

The roads were hilly as we made our way to "Rose Bank". Suddenly, the car stopped and I was told, "We are here." As I looked outside the car window, I saw the gate to the house with the sign that read, "Rose Bank". We rang the doorbell and the housemaid opened the gate just a fraction. Through the crack in the door she talked to the driver in Tamil. I was told that the "masters" of the house had gone to the club and that she did not have their permission to open the gate. I resorted to begging her

A profusion of flowers in the gardens of Rose Bank

Main entrance to Rose Bank, Kodaikanal

to let me in just a little so I could see my teacher's house and take a photograph or two. I promised her I would be quick. She obliged most reluctantly.

There were flowers everywhere! The house is exactly as Mario Montessori had described it. The garden in the front led to a few stairs, which I climbed to get into the house and see the fireplace, and then through the house to the back garden. I could scarcely believe I was standing in the place that had guided my teacher's thinking toward the nature of the relationships among all living things—what we now call cosmic education. As Mario Montessori acknowledges:

> "it was at Kodaikanal where Dr. Montessori developed certain visions and through these visions applied and planned classes for children" (1998, p. 42).

Deprived of their teaching materials, they used the resource that was plentiful in Kodaikanal—nature—and wrote a curriculum that had no boundaries and is still relevant today. It arouses interest and intensifies the child's sense of belonging to the planet through time and space, and hence, Montessori wrote:

> "Let us give the child a vision of the whole universe. The universe is an imposing reality and an answer to all questions. We shall walk together on this path of life, for all things are part of the universe and are connected with each other to form one whole unity" (1989, p. 5-6).

Back at the hotel and expressing my gratitude to the manager, I ventured to ask him how he knew where "Rose Bank" was. He smiled at me and said every house in Kodaikanal is known by its name; that they have no addresses there, just the names of the houses. I was certainly glad that some things haven't changed, and that "Rose Bank" has stayed "Rose Bank" over the years.

With the War coming to a close, Maria Montessori began to make plans for returning to Europe and continuing her teacher training courses. She wrote to her former students in London to make arrangements for her to stay and train teachers. Maria and Mario came back to Amsterdam and were re united with the grandchildren and Ada Pierson who had looked after the children during their time in India. Montessori left for England soon after to continue her work there.

Chapter 12
Maria Montessori in England: "the beginning of a great era for the children"

The gardens of the First Montessori school in England (1914)

By 1912, the Montessori "movement" was rapidly spreading all over the world – schools had opened in Paris, New York, Boston, and "others were about to open in India, China, Mexico, Korea, Honolulu, and the Argentine Republic. A good rail network made European travel increasingly easy, and the Casa dei Bambini in Rome and other Montessori establishments were much visited by educationists from Britain. As the *Times Educational Supplement* described it, the 'pilgrimage to Rome' had become the educationists' 'Grand Tour'" (Cunningham, 2000, p. 210).

Among the people who visited the Casa dei Bambini was Bertram Robert Hawker (1868-1952). He was on his way to Australia to deal with his properties there when he stopped in Rome and was taken by the British Ambassador to see the original Casa dei Bambini. He was so impressed by what he saw that he never made it to Australia. He immediately returned to his home in East Runton, Norfolk, where he opened England's first Montessori school. There were 12 children aged between 3-5 years who were taught by the first Montessori-trained teacher in England, Evelyn Lydbetter (Cunningham, 2000). I met with Barbara Emery whose father George Emery attended the first Montessori school in 1914. He was 3 years old at the time and went there for one and a half years. Barbara says he would talk to her about it, and often when they were on walks, he would point out the school saying, "That's the Montessori school I went to."

Child builds the Pink Tower in Runton (1914) (Runton Parish Council, England)

Soon after, "Montessori schools and classes began to proliferate" (Cohen, p. 56). Photographs of the school illustrated the first edition of *Dr. Montessori's Own Handbook*, which was published in England in 1914.

The first Montessori school in England (1914)

Rev. Hawker was also instrumental in forming the English Montessori Society with the intention of training Montessori teachers for English schools and educating the teaching profession and the public about the method (Kramer, 1988). The first National Conference of the Society was organized from 25-27th July 1914 and the 250 delegates were accommodated in the grounds, buildings, and barn of Rev. Bertram Hawker's house.

Dr. Montessori sent a supporting telegram, which was read by the Chairman, Mr. B.V. Melville, "I associate myself cordially with the Conference in favor of the liberation of the child. Grateful for the recognition of my work." Professor Culverwell from the University of Dublin declared,

"A new light has appeared in the educational world. The remarkable advance made by Dr. Maria Montessori, of Rome, in the theory and practice of the home and school education of children up to seven years of age, will

The barn where the first Montessori conference in 1914 was held

ultimately place her name with those
of Pestalozzi and Froebel as one of the
greatest in the history of educational
progress..." (Cunningham, 2000, p. 211).

The children of the school exhibited the
method. At the end of the conference, Lord
Lytton declared that they should now grow into a
larger, wider organization, embracing Montessori
and kindred movements (Kramer, 1988). This is
just what Dr. Montessori did not want, and she
strongly opposed the idea. She did not want her
pedagogical approach to blend in with any other

Montessori child in
Runton (1914) (Runton
Parish Council,
England)

educational system or to lose control of her methods and materials.
By the end of 1914, the Society split, and when it was reorganized,
Maria Montessori was the President.

In the same spot, Runton Old Hall Garden, London

Plans were made for
Dr. Montessori to come to
London in 1914. However,
with the outbreak of the
First World War, the
plans were shelved and
it was not until 1919 that
she was able to come.
"She was scheduled to
deliver a series of lectures
as well as to preside over
a four-month training
course (Sept.1 – Dec. 20)
in London, and further
to deliver a series of
lectures in twelve other
cities in England" (Cohen,
1974). She received a

Runton Old Hall Garden (2019) and Montessori child in the same spot (1914) (Runton Parish Council, England)

very warm reception during her visit, with newspapers reporting, "That famous woman, pioneer in children's education, Dr. Maria Montessori, arrived in London... to give a training course – her first in this country. The course is limited to an attendance of 250 persons, but over two thousand applications have been made" (Daily News, September 1919). The course was held at St. Bride's Foundation Institute. It included 50 hours of teaching with the training materials, 50 hours of lectures, and 50 hours of observing classes as they operated. It went on to become the standard format for Montessori teacher training that is still used today.

Mrs. Sheila Jamieson Radice, who spent time with Dr. Montessori in London and wrote her impressions and conversations with Montessori in *The New Children: Talks with*

St. Bride's Institute, London

Dr. Maria Montessori, writes, "The first lecture given by Dr. Montessori in this country was delivered before a crowded audience of teachers at St. Bride Foundation, Fleet Street, on the first of September, 1919" (p. 8).

The training was acclaimed as the beginning of a new era for the children of England (Rev. Cecil Grant). There was a demonstration class that was formed by the London County Council and led by Signorina Maccheroni that illustrated the principles that Dr. Montessori expounded in her lectures. "Montessori's lectures were enthusiastically received, and the visit was a great personal triumph" (Cohen, 1974). *The Times* concluded upon Montessori's departure, "She has come, she has been heard, she has largely conquered."

After this, Montessori returned to England every other year, and in 1923, she authorized the establishment of a Montessori training school under the direction of one of her former students, Claude Claremont. These classes were held at "Studio House".

The course was two years in length and culminated with Dr. Montessori giving a four-month course. She was very particular that her teaching method was fully embraced and hence her "students studied nothing but Montessori, by Montessori, with Montessorians. 'We Montessori the students', boasted Claremont" (Cohen, 1974). In 1925, Mario Montessori took the course and received his Montessori Diploma.

In 1936, the Fifth International Montessori Congress was held

Studio House, London

in Oxford, England. It was at this Congress that additional principles for use in Montessori education concerning elementary and high schools were developed. Dr. Montessori said:

"My vision of the future is no longer of people taking exams and proceeding on that certificate form the secondary school to the university, but of individuals passing from one stage of independence to a higher, by means of their own activity, through their own effort of will, which constitutes the inner evolution of the individual" (1989, p. 107).

However, now all her plans had to take the back burner as Europe was in turmoil. This was no time for progressive education or new ideals, and Montessori was hit especially hard. Montessori Societies in Italy, Germany, and Austria were closed, and so were her schools. Montessori herself fled from Italy in 1935 and lived in Barcelona until a British battleship evacuated her to England. From there she traveled with Mario to the Netherlands where she stayed with the family of Ada Pierson

DR. MONTESSORI HOME FROM LECTURE TOUR

Dr. Maria Montessori, founder of the education system which bears her name, being welcomed at the Montessori Training School, Hampstead, by the secretary of the Society after her return from a lecture tour in Europe

The Times – August 12, 1935
(Courtesy of Maria Montessori Training Institute, London England)

(who later became Mario's second wife). She was invited by the Theosophical Society in India to hold a training course in Madras (now Chennai) and with all the doors closing in on her in Europe, she accepted the invitation.. She left Europe for India (November 1939) for three months but with the outbreak of the Second World War it turned out to be a much longer stay. Mario was interned and Maria was put under house arrest.in the Theosophical Society in Adyar (a large neighborhood in South Chennai).

It was not until 1946, after an absence of eight years, that Dr. Montessori once again returned to England. While still in India, Montessori approached two of her former students, Margaret Homfray and Phoebe Child, to organize teacher training for her in London. At the end of the war, this was no easy task and there were many difficulties to overcome before the training could begin. Houses to rent were hard to find, neither had any money, food was being rationed, and there were no teaching materials. Delta Newby writes in *Margaret Homfray: The Spirit of Montessori:*

> "The London to which Dr. Montessori returned in 1946 after an absence of seven years to give what was to be her last course in that city was a very different London from that which she left just before the war... Much of the city had been reduced to rubble, the sky-line was no longer recognizable, food and clothing were severely rationed" (1991, p. 53).

A big house was found on Porchester Terrace in the Hyde Park area and this was ideal as it provided a lecture hall for the students and a residence for Maria Montessori. They borrowed furniture, linen, kitchen equipment, and crockery to make Montessori comfortable, and driving to the airport to pick her up, they felt very satisfied with what they were able to accomplish.

Dr. Montessori had other ideas than just a comfortable abode! As soon as she landed in London she said to Homfray and Child,

Porchester Terrace, London

"Look, this afternoon I want you to get a car and drive me all over London and show me the war damage" (1991, p. 54). After surveying the destruction and returning to Porchester Terrace, Montessori remarked, "Yes, there was a lot of damage, but I saw the Quetta earthquake in India and that was much worse" (1991, p. 55).

Renilde Montessori, granddaughter of Dr. Montessori, writes in the Foreword to The 1946 London Lectures, "This course-in itself an interesting milestone from a historical point of view-was to have unspectacular but profoundly significant pedagogical consequences, since the 1946 Lectures were to become the foundation of all AMI 3-6 courses." The training course was very well attended and was a big success. Annette Haines in the Introduction to *The 1946 London Lectures* says:

> "It is a mature voice, the voice of Dr. Montessori in 1946, six years before her death. As you read, you sense that she has been around the world, from Argentina to Australia, from India to the United States, and has observed, profoundly and scientifically, an immense amount of things, specifically the discoveries made in San Lorenzo – discoveries about the child and the nature of human development – validated over and over again. By 1946, she is totally sure of herself and sure of what she is saying" (2012).

So successful were the lectures that Maria Montessori was in agreement that a permanent training center was needed in London. She gave permission to Margaret Homfray and Phoebe Child to run the courses and that she would sign the diplomas. Montessori wanted an "education trust to be set up in her name to ensure the preservation and continuity of her work of spreading the Philosophy and Method. On this note, at the close of the course, Dr. Montessori returned to Holland" (Newby, 1991, p. 56). This is how the first Montessori Training Center in London began and which later became known as St. Nicholas. The teacher training in London grew rapidly and a nursery school for 120 children aged between two and a half and eleven was started at 33 Chepstow Villas in Notting Hill to give teaching experience to the teachers.

In 1951, Dr. Montessori visited London again for a short time. Newby writes:

> "Now, alert and purposeful, at Chepstow Villas she personally signed diplomas, reiterated her permission for graduates to purchase the treasured silver and enamel brooch of the child "paddling his own canoe" which she herself designed and

Chepstow Villa, London

Gatehouse Montessori, London (1951)

which Margaret and Phoebe had acquired those 21 years before – and again discussed the all-important subject of the educational trust to ensure the continuity of her work which was in the process of being set up" (1991, p. 69).

The trust was set up in 1952 taking the name of St Nicholas, the patron saint of children. It moved to 23 and 24 Prince's Gate in 1969 and remains there to this day.

The Ninth International Montessori Congress was held in London in May 1951 and this was the last one that Maria Montessori attended. There were 150 delegates from seventeen countries that attended the lectures on "Education as an Aid to the Natural Development of the Psyche of the Child from Birth to University". Mario Montessori spoke on the method of education and Dr. Montessori, now 81 years old, spoke on her philosophy of education. There were teachers who she had trained who gave examples on the presentations of the materials. One such teacher was Phyllis Wallbank, a close friend of Dr. Montessori. Mrs. Wallbank founded the Gatehouse Learning Center, the first all-age Montessori school in England, in the sitting room on the first floor of the Gatehouse rectory of St. Bartholomew the Great. Dr. Montessori visited the school several times in her later years, the last being in 1951 when the photo above was taken of the children singing to her.

The little girl sitting next to Maria Montessori is Judith Wolfram (6 years old in the photo), daughter of Phyllis Wallbank.

St Bartholomew the Great Church: site of Gatehouse Montessori, London

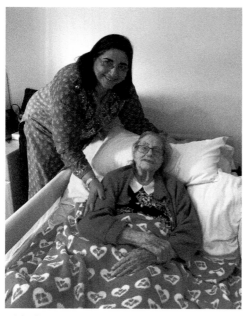

With Phyllis Wallbank

I was fortunate to meet her and hear first hand stories of the Montessoris, Ted Standing, and Claude Claremont, who were frequent visitors to their home.

I also met Phyllis Wallbank in June 2019, now 100 years old, who told me when I asked her what Dr. Montessori was like:

"She was very engrossed in her work and she wanted it everywhere."

The Montessoris had made The Netherlands their home and it was from here that Maria Montessori travelled back and forth giving lectures, addressing UNESCO and receiving the first of her three Nobel Peace Prize nominations.

Acknowledgements:
Barbara Emery, Runton Parish Council
Phyllis Wallbank, London
Judith Wolfram, London
Michael Newman, New Ideals in Education, London
William Macadam, East Runton
Jethryn Hall, Maria Montessori Training Organization, London
Sid Mohandas, London

Chapter 13
Mammolina's Amsterdam Years

Bust of Maria Montessori, Amsterdam.

With the Second World War over, Maria Montessori and her son, Mario, returned from India and came to live in Amsterdam. This was a very busy time for Dr. Montessori, affectionately known as 'Mammolina' by teachers and students "to whom she had become a symbol of hopefulness for humanity, of the kind of optimism necessary to once again rebuild a ravaged world" (Kramer, 1976, p. 350). Now 77 years old, she was constantly on the move, going from one country to another to lecture training courses, and of course to receive honors and rewards. Unlike what she had imagined in India during the War, she was far from forgotten in Europe, which was "once again liberated and once again in a mood of renewal, full of hopes and plans for rebuilding a better world" (Kramer, 1976, p. 360). The significance of Dr. Montessori's work was being realized, and she was nominated for the Nobel Peace Prize in 1949, and then again in 1950 and 1951.

The home that Dr. Montessori chose to live in Amsterdam was to be her last. During my recent visit to Koninginneweg 161, I was told that the charm of this particular house and why it was chosen to be her residence was that it had an elevator that was much needed, as Maria Montessori was now old and frail. The house is beautiful, but it is her study on the second floor that has been largely preserved in its original state, where I sensed I was walking on sacred ground. It is as though her spirit lives on in this bright room with all her original furniture that had been moved from Barcelona.

I tiptoed into the room, scared to put my feet on the gorgeous rug, only to be told to come and sit on the chairs. I could scarcely believe that, but was grateful to be able to sit down and soak it all in.

The walls are adorned with photographs—those of her parents, of herself during different episodes of her life, and one in

Montessori's Study, Amsterdam

particular that caught my attention which is the portrait painted by Sir Frank Salisbury, a renowned British artist. The portrait was given to Mario Montessori in 1955. As Montessorians, we have all seen this beautiful painting of our Mammolina and probably have a framed copy in our schools, but to see the original in her study is something quite different. In the painting, Maria Montessori is wearing a black gown with a pearl string, looking so elegant and dignified while holding a book that reads "Mammolina Immortale" (Immortal Mammolina).

The walls are also decorated with diplomas, certificates, awards, and letters of recognition. My attention focuses on the letter by Rabindranath Tagore, poet, writer, philosopher, and pedagogue from India who was also the first non-European to win the Nobel Prize for literature. He writes to Dr. Montessori in 1940:

In the shadow of my teacher

"As you know, I am a great admirer of your work in education, and along with my countrymen think it is very fortunate indeed that India, at this hour, can get your guidance in creative self-expression. I am confidant that education of the young, which must underlie all work of national reconstruction, will find anew and lasting inspiration from your presence".

It is interesting to note that the diploma awarded by King Umberto I to Maria Montessori on her graduation as a doctor (July 10, 1896) was modified to say "Signora", as she was the first woman in Italy to graduate as a doctor. Similarly, when Mario Montessori obtained his Montessori diploma in London (1925), his certificate was changed from "she" to "he". Both mother and son as ambassadors of change!

The display case in the study holds many of Maria Montessori's medals and awards. I was fortunate enough to be able to hold a few of them. Among them was the gold brooch with the inscription that translates, "To Maria Montessori from her native town." This was presented to her when she visited the place of her birth, Chiaravalle, on August 26, 1950. In a picture close by, she is wearing the brooch during the ceremony.

Gold brooch received by Dr. Montessori in Chiaravalle (1950)

The bookcase in the study contains various titles written by Dr. Montessori herself. There are several editions and languages of the books, including *The Absorbent Mind and The Montessori Method.* There are also books by her followers and admirers who have dedicated their books to her. Next to the mantelpiece, a familiar picture catches my eye and provides me comfort. It is Raphael's *Madonna della Seggiola.* Of this painting that Maria Montessori said every school should have, she wrote:

"In this beautiful conception, Raphael has not only shown us the Madonna as a Divine Mother holding in her arms the baby who is greater than she, but by the side of this symbol of all motherhood, he has placed the figure of St. John, who represents humanity. So in Raphael's picture we see humanity rendering homage to maternity, -maternity, the sublime fact in the definite triumph of humanity" (Montessori, 1912/1964, p. 82).

In Dr. Montessori's Study, Amsterdam

I stand behind her desk and gently run my fingers along it. I can scarcely breathe as I take it all in. This is the desk at which she wrote as my eyes rest on the inkstand and the bottle of Gimborn ink. There is also an ink blotter, which one does not see much of anymore in our age of computers, but I remember it from my childhood. As I pick it up, I can see her beautiful signature blotted on it. There is also a typewriter in the room and I am told it is extremely heavy and that Montessori preferred to write by hand. There are a few boxes on her desk, one looks like a papier-mâché from Kashmir, India, and another is a wooden box with dragons on it, which probably held stamps and papers. There is also an ashtray made of onyx with a matchbox in a leather cover that looks like a book.

With great trepidation, I ask if I could sit in her chair and I am told I may, just because I asked so politely. As I do so, I am filled with gratitude for this woman who has given my life direction and purpose. I pledge again to follow her principles with integrity and do my best to serve the child. There are fresh flowers on her desk, for the day that I am visiting is her birthday. How perfect!

Maria Montessori's "long and self-sacrificing labours on behalf of the child – and through him of humanity – ended suddenly on 6th May 1952 at Noordwijk-on-Sea, in Holland" (Standing, 1957, p. 72). She was eighty-one years old and had kept a demanding

House by the Sea, Noordwich

work schedule, traveling and lecturing in international congresses in Italy, France, Austria, England, and Scotland. As customary, Montessori had come to Noordwijk to spend a couple of weeks in the summer home of Ada Pierson's family. She was sitting with Mario in *Het Huis aan Zee (The House at the Sea)*, the summerhouse of the Pierson family, and was thinking of taking a trip to Africa to give a lecture. It was suggested that she was too weak to travel and perhaps someone else should go in her place. Dr. Montessori turned to Mario and said, "Am I no longer of any use then?" (Kramer, 1976, p. 367). She died shortly afterward of cerebral hemorrhage.

Dr. Montessori considered herself to be a citizen of the world and had always said she wished to be buried where she died. In accordance with her wishes, she was interred in the courtyard of the Catholic cemetery at Gooweg. Her grandson, Mario Montessori Junior, designed her grave. The epitaph in Italian reads: *I ask the lovely children that can do everything to help me to build peace among people and in the world.*

Montessori's grave in Gooweg

Acknowledgements:
Joke Verheul, Association Montessori Internationale,
The Netherlands
Fred Kelpin, Montessori Pedagog.

AFTERWORD

Child of Peace (Heping) statue at Montessori Casa
International, Denver

Following Maria Montessori's journey around the world with all the trials and tribulations she experienced, the one thing I found that remained constant and provided her with undying faith was her belief that "the child was both a promise and hope for mankind" (1992). It was in 1937, during the Sixth International Montessori Congress in Copenhagen, that Maria Montessori said,

> "The child today is a 'forgotten citizen'; society must now turn its attention to him and create an environment that will fulfill his vital needs and foster his spiritual liberation" (1992, p. 38).

Montessori did this, as we know, in San Lorenzo in 1907, where she made the momentous discovery that when children were allowed to develop according to their natural plan, they were industrious, responsible, orderly, self-disciplined, joyful, happy, calm, and peaceful. In addition, they were "contributing members of their society" (1992). Let's be honest, unfortunately these are not characteristics we currently associate with children..

What had caused this change in the children? When the children are free in an environment that is set up to meet their needs and they are allowed to choose purposeful work from their own spontaneous motivation, peace is naturally manifested. Peace, as conceptualized by Maria Montessori, is not confined to a place... an exercise... a syllabus item. She understood that peace could not be brought about by demonstrations or taught through a curriculum. A peaceful society cannot emerge from peace talks, yoga mornings, or mediation retreats, but from a foundation that integrates body, mind, and spirit. What we need is an education that nurtures the whole person, not simply giving facts, passing down formal knowledge and teaching to the test. As Montessori so famously said:

> "Establishing lasting peace is the work of education; all politics can do is keep us out of war" (1992, p. 24).

A devoted humanitarian, she was nominated three times for the Nobel Peace Prize for her efforts toward a more peaceful society.

Dr. Montessori's journey is an inspiring one. Not only did she revolutionize education, but also worked to further the rights of women and children and of all humankind. She worked tirelessly to create a better world, confident in the ability of the child to create a more peaceful, harmonious society. Let us rededicate ourselves and continue her legacy, knowing that,

The three hour uninterrupted work cycle at Montessori Casa International, Denver CO

"the child constructs himself, that he has a teacher within himself and that this inner teacher also follows a programme and a technique of education, and that we adults by acknowledging this unknown teacher may enjoy the privilege and good fortune of becoming its assistants and faithful servants by helping it with our co-operation" (1989, p. 46).

I, for one, have undertaken this journey following Maria Montessori's footsteps with the purpose of understanding her philosophy and methodology better. It stems from my desire to provide an education for the children of my school that is as true to her principles as possible.

BIBLIOGRAPHY

Cavini, D. (2013). *Storia di Alice che fu la talent-scout di Maria Montessori* Città di Castello: Pioniere dell'educazione.

Cohen, S. (1974). *The Montessori Movement in England, 1911-1952.* History of Education: Journal of the history of Education Society, 3:1, 51-67.

Cunningham, P. (2011). *The Montessori phenomenon: Gender and internationalism in early twentieth-century innovation* in Practical Visionaries: Women, Education and Social Progress 1790-1930 by Mary Hilton and Pam Hirsch.

Fisher, D.C. (1912). *A Montessori mother.* Henry Holt & Company, New York.

Gutek, G.L. (2004). *The Montessori Method. The origins of an educational innovation: Including an Abridged and Annotated Edition of Maria Montessori's The Montessori Method.* New York: Rowman and Littlefield Publishers.

Gutek, G.L. & Gutek, P.A. (2016). *Bringing Montessori to America.* The University of Alabama Press, Tuscaloosa.

Kahn, D. *"The Kodaikanal Experience: Kahn-Montessori Interview"* (Reprinted The NAMTA Journal Spring 1998).

Kahn, D. *"The Kodaikanal Experience: Kahn-Wikramaratnei Interview"* (Reprinted The NAMTA Journal Winter 2013).

Kramer, R. (1976). *Maria Montessori: A biography.* New York: Putnam.

Lillard, A. S. (2005). *Montessori: The science behind the genius.* New York: Oxford University Press.

Maccheroni, A.M. (1947). *A true romance: Dr. Maria Montessori as I knew her*. The Darien Press, Edinburgh.

McClure, S.S. (1911). *McClure's Magazine: Illustrated, published monthly May to October, 1911*. SS McClure Company, New York & London.

Montessori, M. (1912/1964). *The Montessori method*. New York: Schocken.

Montessori, M. (1948/1973). *From Childhood to Adolescence*. New York: Schocken Books.

Montessori, M. (1949). *The San Remo Lectures, 1949*. Association Montessori Internationale.

Montessori, M. (1965). *Dr. Montessori's own handbook*. New York: Schocken Books.

Montessori, M.(1966). *The secret of childhood*. New York: Ballantine Books

Montessori, M. (1970). *How it all happened: Dr. Montessori Speaks* AMI Communication, 1970, no 2/3, p. 4.

Montessori, M. (1988). *The absorbent mind*. Oxford, England: Clio Press: England.

Montessori, M. (1989). *Education for a new world*. Clio Press.

Montessori, M. (1989). *The child in the family*. Clio Press: England.

Montessori, M. (1989). *The formation of man*. Clio Series.

Montessori, M. (1989). *To educate the human potential*. Clio Series.

Montessori, M. (1992). *Education and peace*. Clio Press: England.

Montessori, M. *"The Impact of India."* (Reprinted The NAMTA Journal Spring 1998).

Montessori, M. (2004). *The discovery of the child.* Oxford, England: Clio Press: England.

Montessori, M. (2004). *The Montessori Method.* New York: Rowman & Littlefield Publishers.

Montessori, M. (2005). *An Anthology.* Association Montessori Internationale, The Netherlands.

Montessori, M. (2008). *The California lectures of Maria Montessori, 1915.* Montessori-Pierson Publishing Company, The Netherlands.

Montessori, M., (2012). *The 1946 London lectures.* Montessori-Pierson Publishing Company, The Netherlands.

Montessori, M. (2013). *Maria Montessori sails to America: A private diary, 1913.* Montessori-Pierson Publishing Company, The Netherlands.

Montessori, M. (2013). *The 1913 Rome lectures: First international training course.* Montessori-Pierson Publishing Company, The Netherlands.

Montessori, M. (2015). *Maria Montessori writes to her father: Letters from California, 1915.* Montessori-Pierson Publishing Company, The Netherlands.

Montessori, M. (2019). *Citizen of the world: Key Montessori readings.* Montessori-Pierson Publishing Company, The Netherlands.

Newby, D. (1991). *Margaret Homfray: The spirit of Montessori.* Multi-Task Business Services, USA.

Pollard, M. (1990). *Maria Montessori: The Italian doctor who revolutionized the education systems of the world*. Exley Publications Ltd, Great Britain.

Povell, P. (2010). *Montessori comes to America*. University Press of America, Maryland.

Radice, S. (1920). *The new children: Talks with Dr. Maria Montessori*. Frederick A. Stokes, New York.

Rubi, F.C., & Garcia, B.S. (2011). The photography and propaganda of Maria Montessori method in Spain (1911-1931). *Paedagogica Historica,* 48 (4), 571–587.

Standing, E. M. (1957). *Maria Montessori: Her life and work*. New York: Plume.

Standing, E.M. (1966). *The Montessori Revolution in Education*. Schocken Books, New York.

Trabalzini, P. (2011). *Maria Montessori through the seasons of the "Method"*. The NAMTA Journal, 36 (2).

Waltuch, M.R. (1986). A Montessori Album: Reminiscences of a Montessori life. Ohio: NAMTA.

White, J.W. (1914). *Montessori schools as seen in the early summer of 1913*. Oxford University Press, London.

Archives

Archive Opera Nazionale Montessori, Rome
Maria Montessori Archives, Amsterdam
Runton Parish Hall, England
Societa Umanitaria Archives, Milan
Hallgarten-Franchetti Foundation Archives, Città di Castello

ABOUT THE AUTHOR

Inspired by Dr. Maria Montessori's philosophy, Punum Bhatia, PhD has dedicated her life to Montessori education as a parent, teacher, and teacher educator for over thirty years. She completed her bachelor's degree in English Literature, earned a master's degrees in English Literature and Education from the University of Calcutta, and completed a certificate diploma in Montessori Pedagogy. She earned her Doctor of Philosophy from the University of Colorado Denver in 2012 for her work on the Self-Efficacy of Montessori teachers. In her efforts to understand children and the environments necessary for them to grow and flourish, Punum focuses on Maria Montessori's original philosophy and techniques. After teaching the Montessori method to cohorts all around the world, she is now the proud owner of her very own bilingual preschool, Montessori Casa International, in Denver, Colorado. She is the author of *A Montessori Workbook*, Volumes 1, 2, 3 and *The Inspired Child* (www.mcidenver.edu/www.punumbhatia.com).